Book 1

BRAIN STRETCHERS

Carolyn Anderson & Jackie Haller

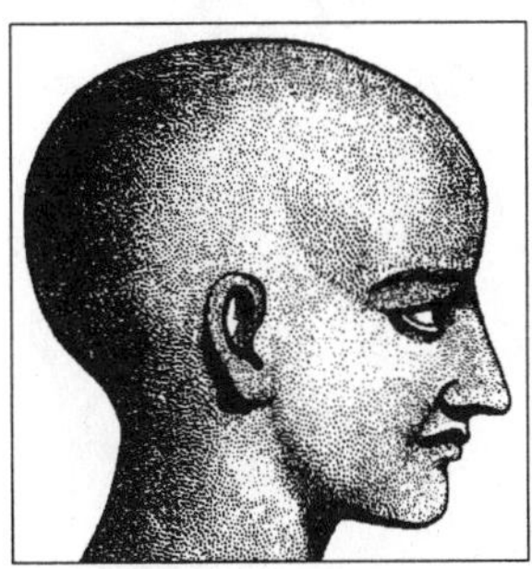

© 1975

CRITICAL THINKING BOOKS & SOFTWARE

www.criticalthinking.com

P.O. Box 448 • Pacific Grove • CA 93950-0448

Phone 800-458-4849 • FAX 831-393-3277

ISBN 0-89455-644-4

Printed in the United States of America

FOREWARD

BRAIN STRETCHERS offers a wide variety of 60 pages of puzzles to help develop <u>critical thinking</u> in your classroom. The materials are roughly <u>middle school</u> complexity but since they are <u>non graded</u>, they may be used anywhere from <u>upper elementary</u> to <u>high school</u>, depending on student needs. Reading levels vary from <u>no read</u> to <u>lo read</u> which will help <u>poor readers</u>, <u>bilinguals</u>, <u>lower</u> verbals and some <u>special eds</u>. The puzzles may be used for <u>individualization</u>, <u>independent work</u>, <u>motivation</u> and <u>enrichment</u>.

Table of Contents

Which one is different?

Which one is different?

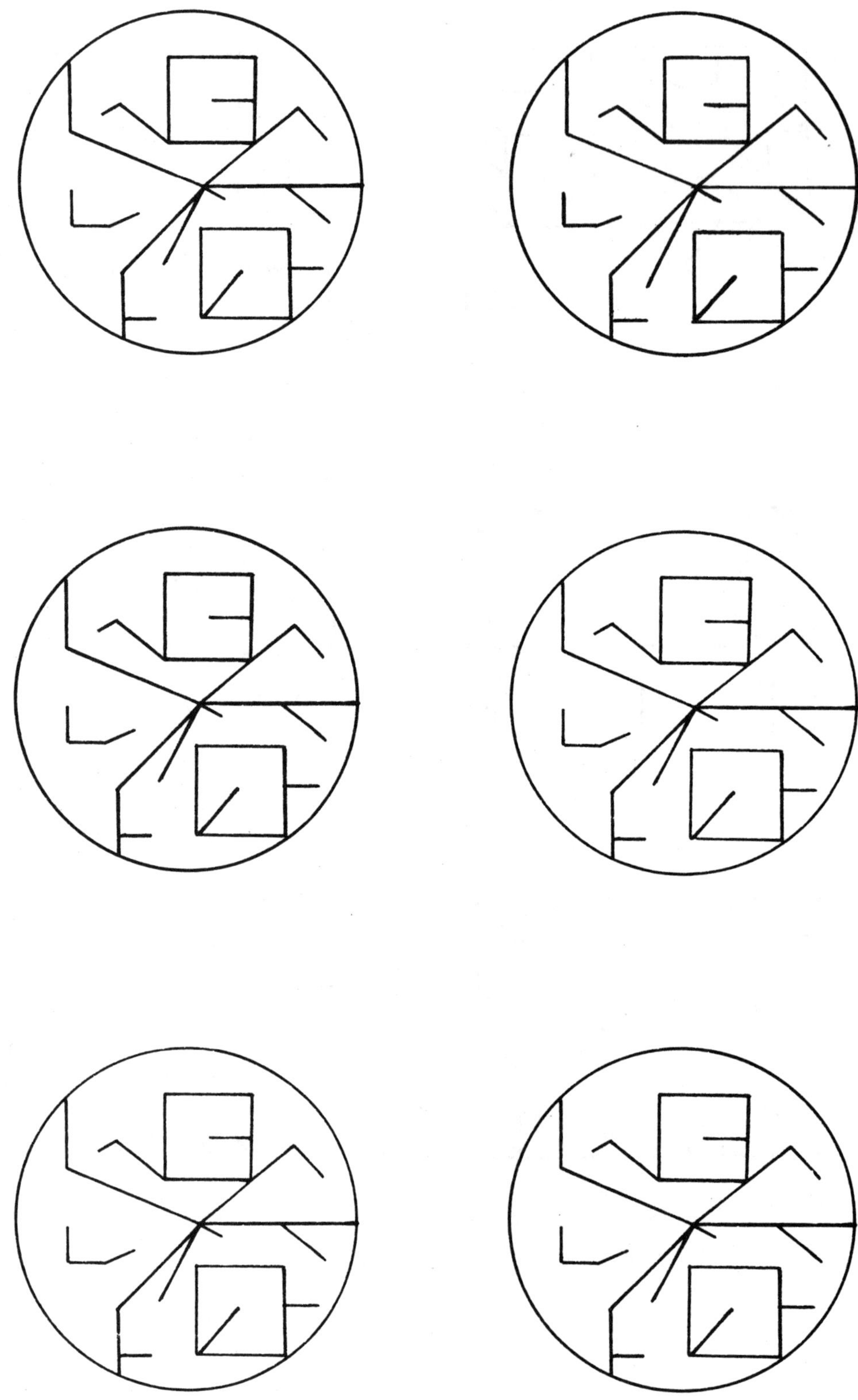

Which one is different?

Figure out the pattern then write the next 3 terms in the series.

1. 1, 2, 6, 24, 120, ___, ___, ___

2. 15, 20, 13, 18, 11, ___, ___, ___

3. 0, 0, 4, 9, 8, 18, 12, 27, ___, ___, ___

4. 2, 3, 5, 8, 9, 11, 14, 15, ___, ___, ___

5. 3, 4, 6, 11, 12, 14, 20, 21, 23, 30, ___, ___, ___

6. 1, 4, 9, 16, 25, ___, ___, ___

7. 1, 8, 27, 64, 125, ___, ___, ___

8. 1, 2, 2, 6, 3, 12, 4, 20, 5, ___, ___, ___

9. 10, 1, 11, 2, 13, 4, 17, 8, 25, 7, ___, ___, ___

10. 98, 72, 77, 49, 54, 20, ___, ___, ___

Figure out the pattern then write the next 3 terms in
the series.

1. 0, 2, 5, 10, 17, 28, 41, 58, ___, ___, ___

2. 1, 2, 4, 7, 8, 10, 25, 26, 28, 79, ___, ___, ___

3. 2, 3, 10, 12, 13, 20, 21, ___, ___, ___

4. 2, 3, 4, 5, 6, 7, 8, 11, 9, 19, 10, ___, ___, ___

5. 0, 2, 4, 0, 3, 6, 0, 4, 8, 0, 5, 10, ___, ___, ___

6. 50, 40, 31, 23, 16, ___, ___, ___

7. 33, 34, 40, 41, 42, 43, 44, 100, 101, 102, ___, ___, ___

8. J, F, M, A, M, J, J, A, S, ___, ___, ___

9. A, Z, B, Y, C, X, D, W, E, V, ___, ___, ___

10. S, H, I, U, X, N, T, D, E, R, E, ___, ___, ___

Figure out the pattern then write the next 3 terms in the series.

1. 2, 3, 5, 7, 11, 13, ___, ___, ___

2. 1, 1, 4, 36, 576, 14,300, ___, ___, ___

3. 3, 6, 12, 15, 30, 33, 66, ___, ___, ___

4. 1, 5, 4, 13, 9, 25, 16, 41, 25, ___, ___, ___

5. 1, 2, 6, 12, 36, 72, ___, ___, ___

6. $1/2$, $1/3$, $2/9$, $4/27$, $8/81$, ___, ___, ___

7. $1\,1/6$, $1\,1/2$, $1\,5/6$, $2\,1/6$, $2\,1/2$, ___, ___, ___

8. 1, $1/2$, $1/6$, $1/24$, $1/120$, ___, ___, ___

9. 5, $1\,2/3$, 8, 2, 12, $2\,2/5$, 17, $2\,5/6$, 23, $3\,2/7$,

                                        ___, ___, ___

10. .101, .1001, .10001, ___, ___, ___

This puzzle is called a magic square! It's magic
because the numbers in each row, each column, and
each of the two diagonals add up to the same number.
In the 3 by 3 square below you are to use the
numbers 5, 10, 15, 20, 25, 30, 35, 40, and 45. Use
each number once and only once. The sum of the rows,
columns, and diagonals should be 75!!

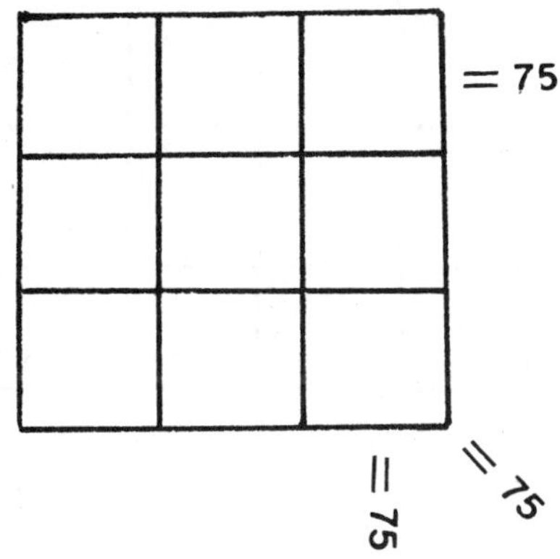

This is a 4 by 4 magic square. You are to use the odd
numbers from 1 to 31 (1, 3, 5, 7, ..., 31). Use each
number once and only once. Each column, each row, and
each of the two diagonals should add up to 64!!

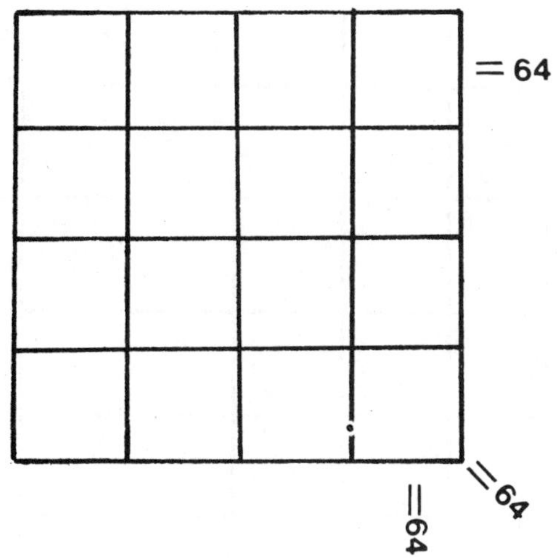

This puzzle is called a magic square! It's magic
because the numbers in each row, each column, and
each of the two diagonals add up to the same number.
In the 4 by 4 below you are to use the multiples of
5 from 5 to 80 (5, 10, 15, ..., 75, 80). The magic
sum of the rows, columns, and diagonals is 170!!

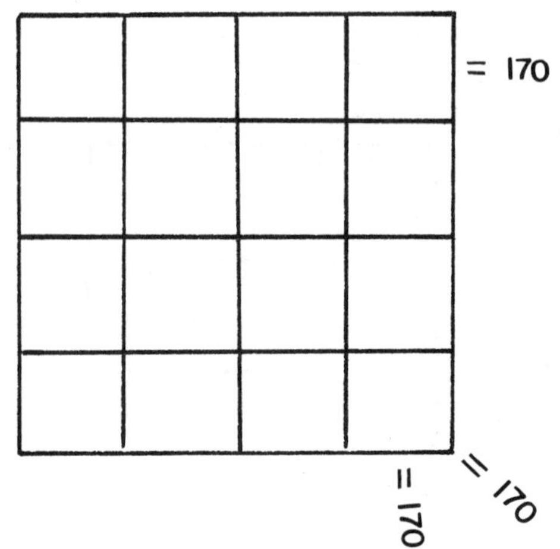

This is a 5 by 5 magic square. You are to use the
even numbers from 2 through 50 (2, 4, 6, ..., 48, 50).
Use each number once and only once. The magic sum for
the rows, columns, and diagonals is 130!!

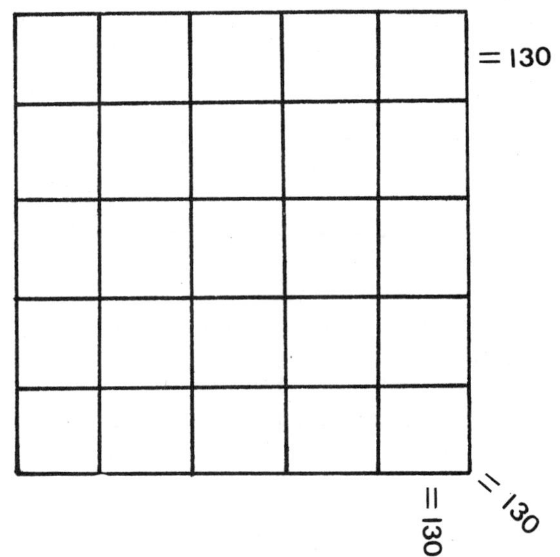

The magic sum in this 5 by 5 magic square is 65! You
are to use the numbers from 1 through 25 (1, 2, ..., 25).

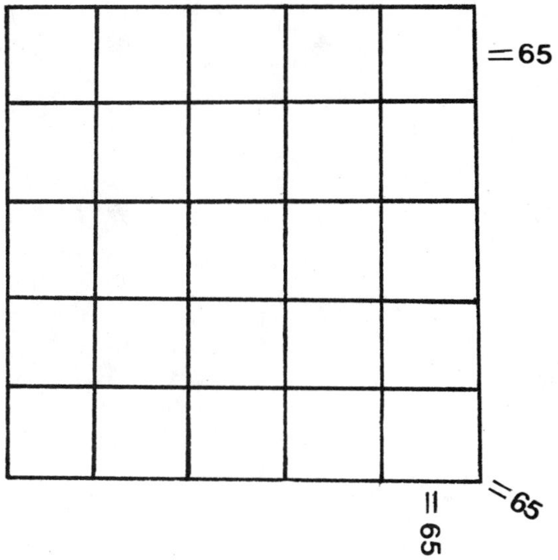

This magic square is an 8 by 8. It's a little tougher
than a 5 by 5 so some of the numbers have been put in
to get you started. You are to use the numbers from 1
through 64 (1, 2, 3, ..., 63, 64). The magic sum is 260!

64			61	60			57	=260
9		54	12	13	51	50	16	
		46			43			
40	26	27		36	30	31	33	
32			29	28			25	
		22	44		19			
			52			10		
8			5	4			1	

Without lifting your pencil, see if you can cross each
dot below using five and only five lines!! Each time you
make a corner, you make a new line and you may cover a
line only once.

Cover the dots below using only six lines. You may not
lift your pencil and each line may be covered only once.

Without lifting your pencil, see if you can cross each
dot below using seven and only seven lines. You may
touch each dot only once and you may not retrace a line.

You are to cover each of the dots below using exactly
eight lines. There are three rules to follow: touch
each dot only once, do not lift your pencil, and do not
trace a line more than once!

Using only eight lines, see if you can cover the dots
below. Here are the rules: do not lift your pencil,
trace each line only once, and touch each dot only one
time!

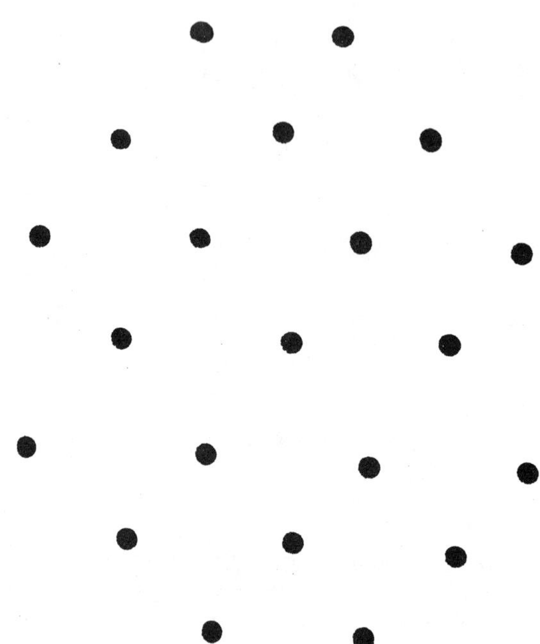

The dots below can be covered using seven and only
seven lines. See if you can do it without lifting
your pencil, without tracing a line more than once,
and without touching a dot more than once.

Given the 11 numbers below, see where they would go in
the cross-number puzzle.

24	125	3525
25	132	4335
54	251	5435
	321	
	451	

Below you are given 12 numbers. See if you can fit
them into the cross-number puzzle.

24	43	256	435
27	46	322	756
32	52	324	
	53		

All 30 of the numbers below will fit into the cross-number puzzle. To get you started one number has been put in for you. See how long it takes you to put in the other 29!!

11	561
12	573
15	721
24	723
39	827
47	912
66	1375
92	1465
93	2163
	3215
	4128
213	6813
291	8324
296	8671
368	8963
425	67825

In the puzzle below you are to fill in the 23 numbers written down each side. One number has been placed for you. See if you can fill in the rest.

22	576
27	629
32	635
54	742
81	918
87	3971
92	4531
	5162
147	8691
191	21352
429	28321
545	87366

There are only 13 numbers that are to be placed in the
cross-number puzzle below.

23	49	81	15463
32	59	89	35781
36	74	726	36178
			69215

In the very special sun glasses below you are to fill
in 24 numbers. Some of the numbers may be filled in
automatically as you fill in the ones around them.
Some of the digits have been placed to give you a start.

26	28324
38	32753
42	34234
45	49528
71	52786
73	56917
82	61852
92	63154
14263	64818
16432	69614
17421	78298
23278	85329

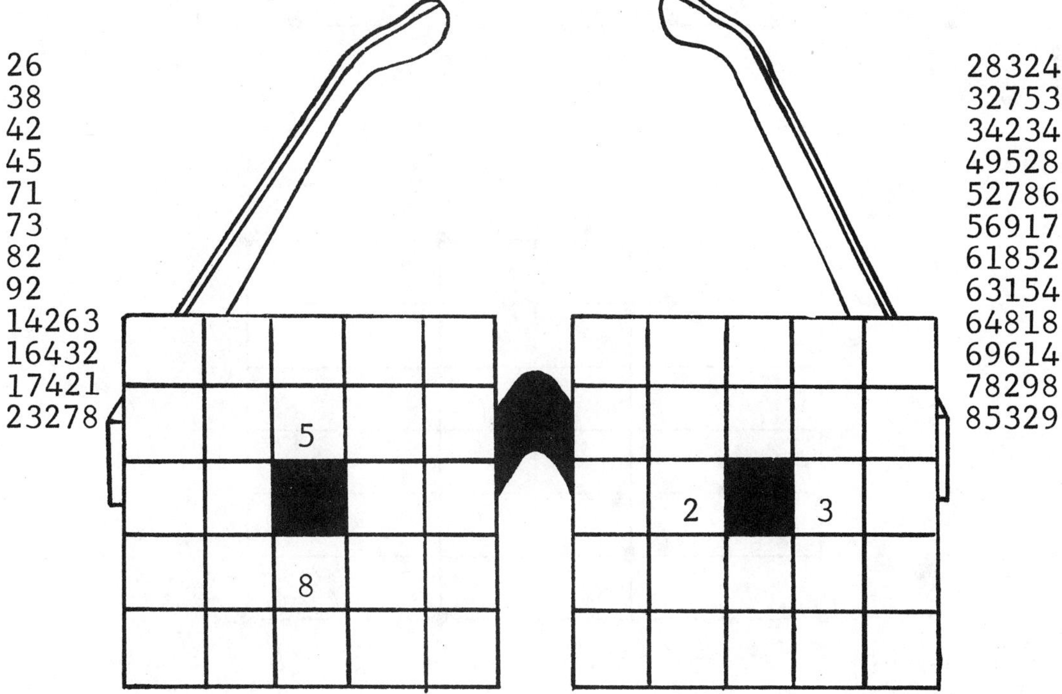

In the pictures below, there are two of each number.
Can you connect them by only moving along the lines
of the grid? No path may touch or intersect another.

Example:

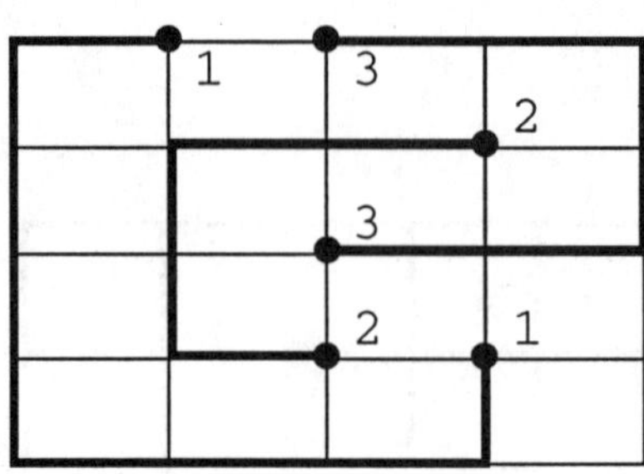

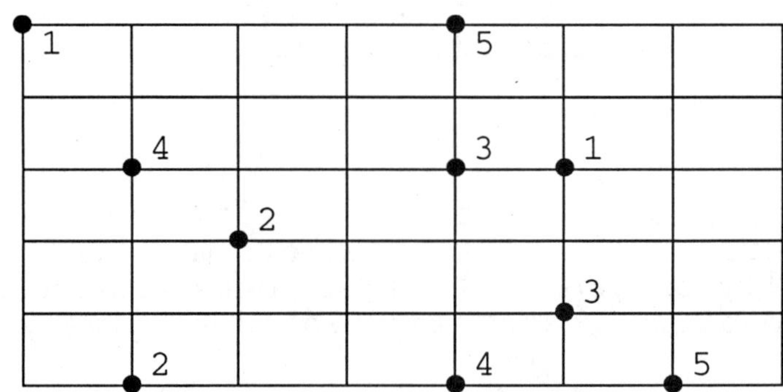

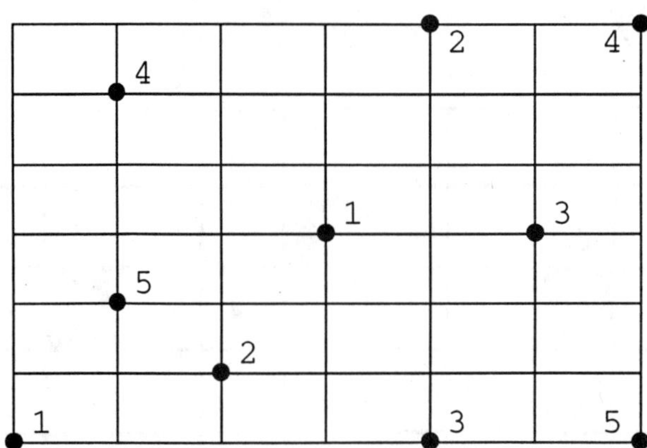

In the pictures below, there are two of each number.
Can you connect them by only moving along the lines
of the grid? No path may touch or intersect another.

Example:

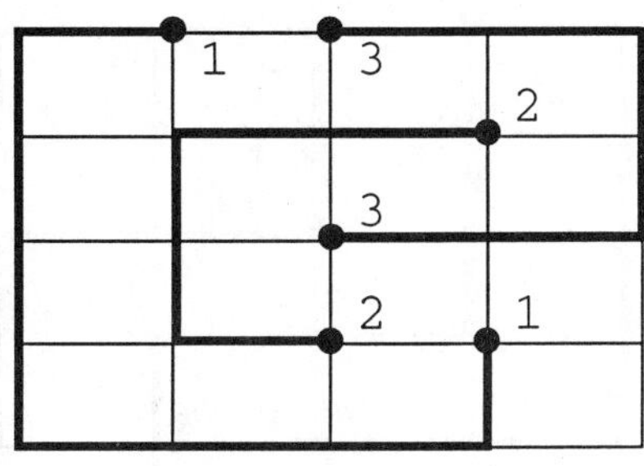

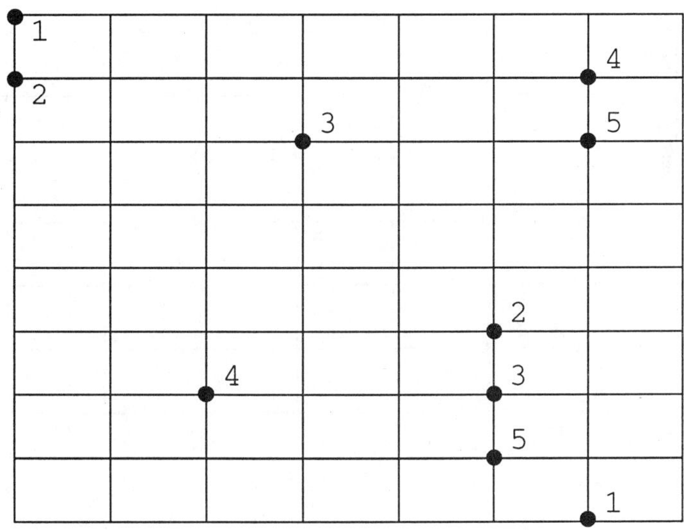

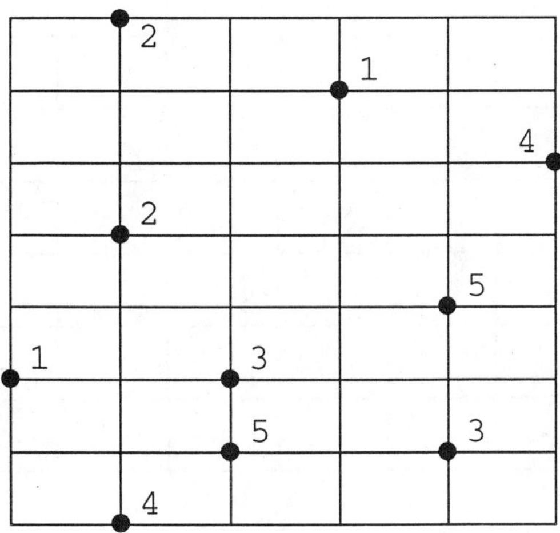

In the pictures below, there are two of each number.
Can you connect them by only moving along the lines
of the grid? No path may touch or intersect another.

Example:

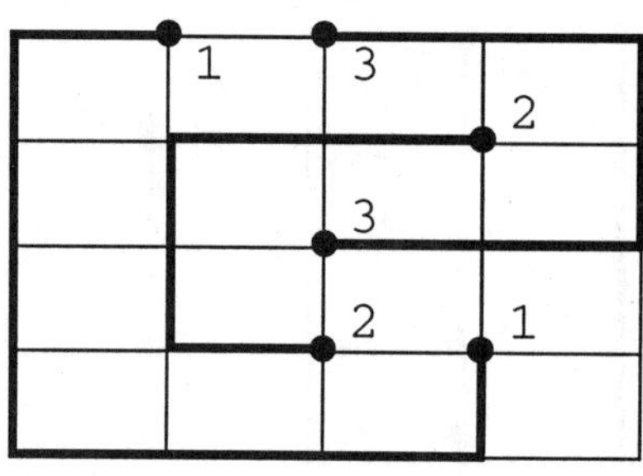

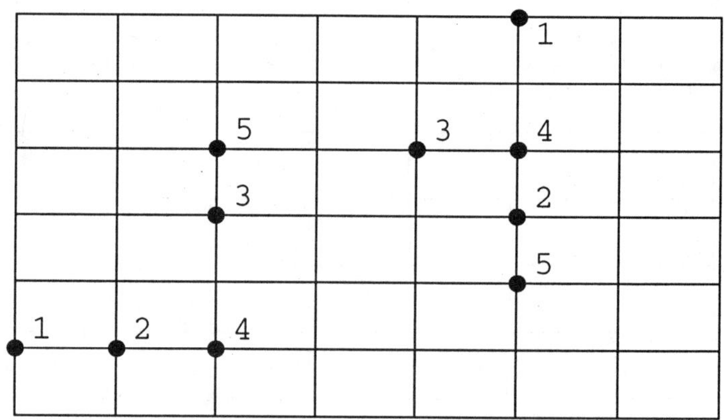

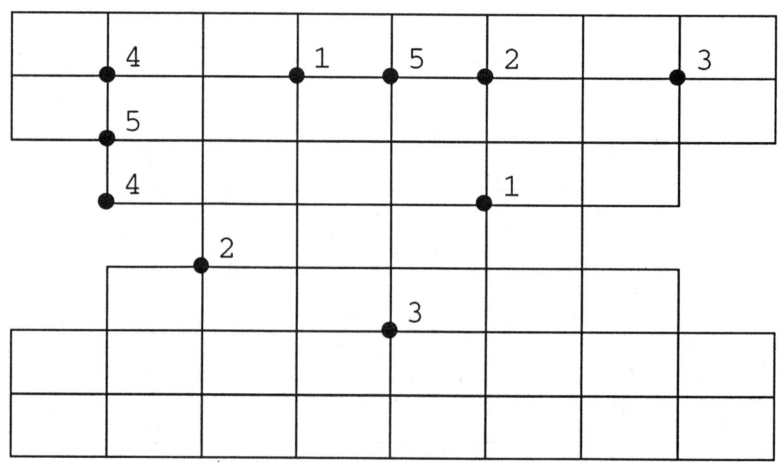

In this cross-number puzzle the definitions for the blanks
give you the sum of the numbers that fill the squares.
That is, the numbers that fill #1 across must add up to
9. There is only one rule--<u>No</u> zeros are allowed!

ACROSS
1.   9
4. 13
6. 14
7. 11
9.   7
11. 15

DOWN
1.   9
2.   5
3. 15
4.   7
5.   9
7. 14
10.   6

This is an addition cross-number. The numbers you use to
fill the squares must add up to the number given in the
definition. There is only one digit allowed per square,
but zeros are not acceptable.

ACROSS
1.   6
3.   5
4.   9
6.   7
8.   8
10. 17
12. 16
13. 5
14. 7
15. 15
17. 10

DOWN
1.   6
2. 10
5.   7
6.   8
7. 18
9.   7
11. 13
14. 18
15. 9
16. 5

The numbers you put in the squares below must add up to
the number given in the definition. That is, the numbers
in the two blanks for #1 across must add up to eight. See
how long it takes you to fill the puzzle!! Do Not use zero!

ACROSS
1.   8
3.   2
5. 12
6. 16
7. 18
9. 10
11. 15
12. 8
14. 19
16. 11

DOWN
1. 15
2. 11
3.   6
4. 17
5.   7
6.   5
8. 16
10. 16
13. 12
14. 9
15. 3
17. 8

Fill the blanks so that the sum of the numbers you use
matches the number given in the definition. No zeros
are allowed.

ACROSS
2. 12
4.   7
5. 10
7.   8
9. 10
11. 3
12. 20
13. 4
14. 18
16. 10
17. 14
19. 9
20. 16

DOWN
1. 10
2.   4
3.   9
4.   9
6.   9
7. 13
8.   4
10. 14
15. 17
16. 11
18. 13
19. 6
21. 14

In an addition cross-number puzzle you are to fill the squares so the sum of the numbers you use is the same as the number given in the definition. Only one number per square and <u>no</u> zeros!

ACROSS
2. 19
4. 9
6. 19
8. 9
10. 2
11. 11
15. 14
19. 27

DOWN
1. 10
2. 18
3. 12
5.   7
7.   4
9.   8
12. 14
13. 18
14. 4
16. 7
17. 12
18. 13
20. 14

Fill the squares so the sums of the numbers match   the sums given in the definitions. Zeros are not allowed!

ACROSS
1.   2
4. 16
6. 19
9.   7
11. 15
13. 10
16. 10
18. 15
19. 3
21. 11
23. 12
24. 3
26. 10
27. 22

DOWN
1.   6
2.   9
3. 27
4. 10
5.   8
7.   6
8.   9
10. 9
12. 14
14. 6
15. 8
17. 16
19. 9
20. 8
22. 23
23. 8
24. 7
25. 6

1. Place one add sign and two subtract signs between the numbers to make the left side of the equation equal 15.

    4   2   4   1   2   4   =   15

2. Place one add sign and one subtract sign between the numbers to make the left side of the equation equal 16.

    6   4   2   3   2   =   16

3. Place two subtract signs and one add sign between the numbers to make the left side of the equation equal 14.

    9   6   3   2   2   1   =   14

4. Place two add signs and two subtract signs between the numbers to make the left side of the equation equal 12.

    2   4   3   1   2   3   =   12

5. Place two add signs and two subtract signs between the numbers to make the left side of the equation equal 24.

    8   6   2   4   4   2   =   24

6. Place two add signs and two subtract signs between the numbers to make the left side of the equation equal 41.

    9   3   6   2   3   1   =   41

7. Place one add sign and two subtract signs between the numbers to make the left side of the equation equal 8.

    1   2   1   2   1   2   =   8

8. Place two add signs and one subtract sign between the numbers to make the left side of the equation equal 6.

    3   2   1   3   2   1   =   6

1. Place one add sign and two division signs between the numbers to make the left side of the equation equal 6.

   3 2 1 1 2 3 = 6

2. Place two add signs and one division sign between the numbers to make the left side of the equation equal 15.

   1 2 3 3 2 1 = 15

3. Place two add signs and two subtraction signs between the numbers to make the left side of the equation equal 0.

   6 5 4 3 2 = 0

4. Place one subtraction sign and one division sign between the numbers to make the left side of the equation equal 10.

   12 6 4 3 2 = 10

5. Place one add, one subtraction, and one division sign between the numbers to make the left side of the equation equal 19.

   1 2 3 4 5 6 = 19

6. Place one subtraction sign and one division sign between the numbers to make the left side of the equation equal 15.

   4 2 4 4 2 8 = 15

7. Place one add, one subtraction, and one division sign between the numbers to make the left side of the equation equal 61.

   6 5 4 4 5 6 = 61

8. Place one add, two subtraction, and one division sign between the numbers to make the left side of the equation equal 3.

   2 3 4 4 3 2 = 3

1. Place one add, two multiplication, and one division
    sign between the numbers to make the left side of
    the equation equal 4.

    3 2 1 2 2 = 4

2. Place two add signs and one division sign between
    the numbers to make the left side of the equation
    equal 9.

    4 2 4 2 2 = 9

3. Place two subtract, one multiplication, and two
    division signs between the numbers to make the
    left side of the equation equal 13.

    24 12 6 3 2 1 = 13

4. Place one add, one subtract, and one division sign
    between the numbers to make the left side of the
    equation equal 32.

    16 8 4 2 1 2 = 32

5. Place three add signs and one division sign between
    the numbers to make the left side of the equation
    equal 5.

    4 2 2 4 2 4 = 5

6. Place two add, one subtraction, and one division
    sign between the numbers to make the left side of
    the equation equal 21.

    24 12 6 4 2 2 = 21

7. Place one add, one multiplication, and one division
    sign between the numbers to make the left side of
    the equation equal 50.

    16 8 4 2 4 = 50

8. Place one subtraction and three multiplication signs
    between the numbers to make the left side of the
    equation equal 36.

    24 12 6 3 2 2 = 36

Each dot represents a warehouse. A watchman must walk
each of the 32 paths between the warehouses. Can you
see how he did it only going over 4 paths twice?
Therefore, when he finished his walk, he would have
walked over 36 paths. (diagonal paths are excluded)

Example: There are 12 paths between the warehouses
           but the watchman will have to walk over 14
           paths to complete his walk.

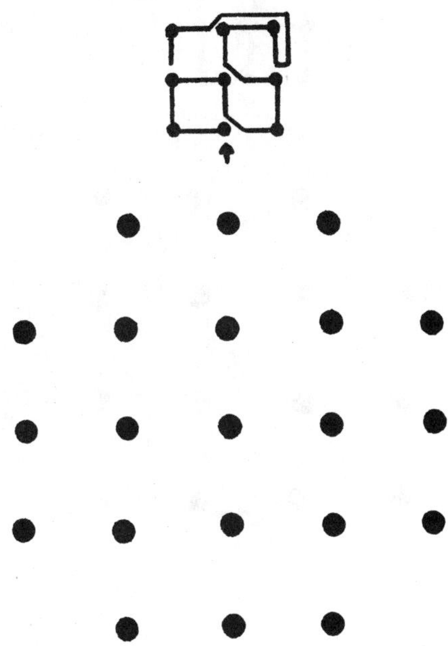

Can you see how the watchman walked over the following
34 paths only going over 4 paths twice.

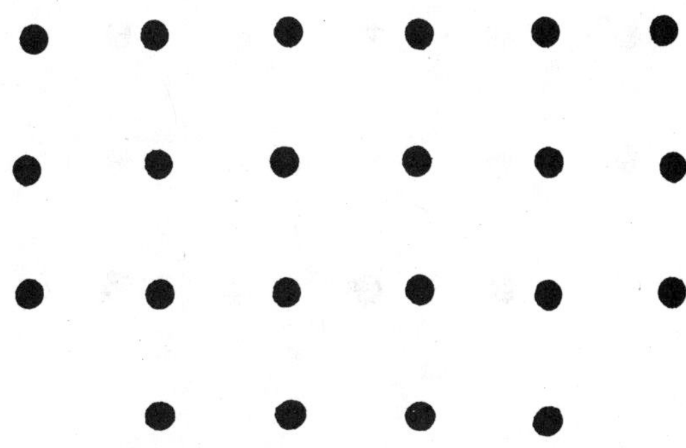

Each dot represents a warehouse. A watchman must walk
each of the 24 paths between the warehouses. Can you
see how he did it only going over 3 paths twice?
Therefore, when he finished his walk, he would have
walked over 27 paths. (diagonal paths are excluded)

Example: There are 12 paths between the warehouses
          but the watchman will have to walk over 14
          paths to complete his walk.

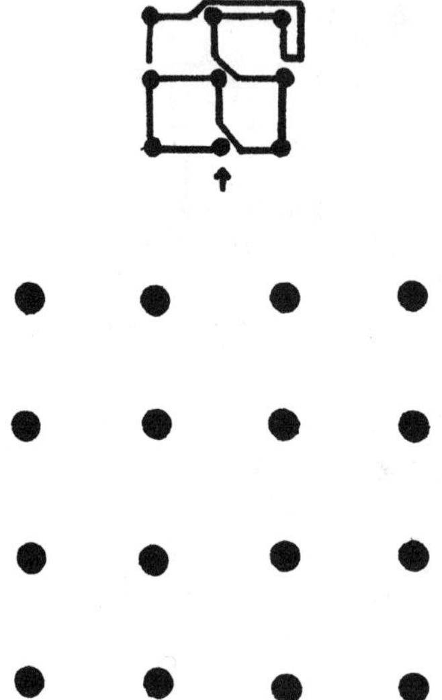

Can you see how the watchman walked over the following
31 paths only going over 4 twice?

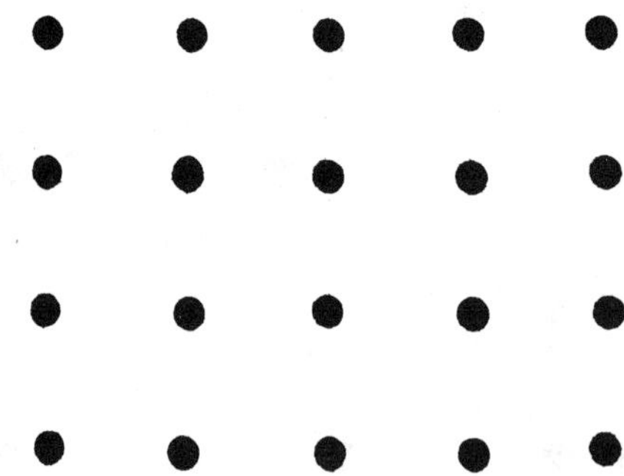

Each dot represents a warehouse. A watchman must walk
each of the 34 paths between the warehouses. Can you
see how he did it only going over 4 paths twice?
Therefore, when he finished his walk, he would have
walked over 38 paths. (diagonal paths are excluded)

Example: There are 12 paths between the warehouses
           but the watchman will have to walk over 14
           paths to complete his walk.

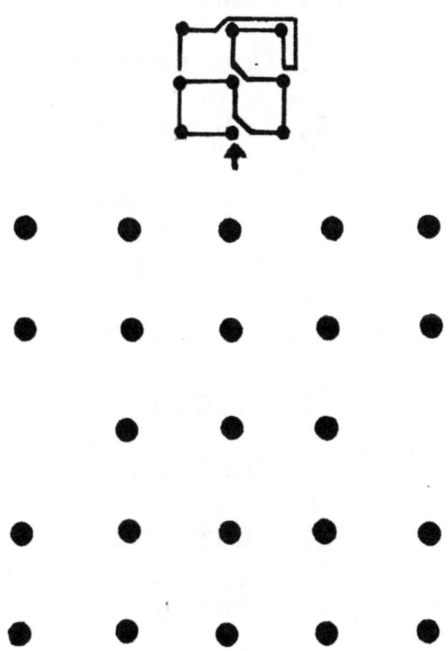

Can you see how the watchman walked over the following
37 paths only going over 5 paths twice?

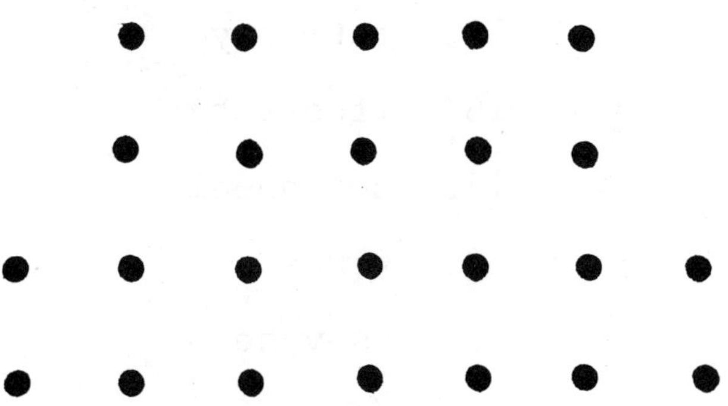

Try to unscramble the following words. Each one of
them is a number (one, eleven, etc.). Careful, some
need hyphens.

1. reoz

2. onneettyw

3. thryit

4. fwoytift

5. ghytie

6. fytfi

7. tgeih

8. netyin

9. ddrenhu

10. ewtvel

11. txysi

12. eeelnv

13. rtofy

14. eeennnti

15. tttwwenyo

16. ffoorruty

17. notyneeni

18. vense

19. tsevyne

Unscramble the following words which are vocabulary
used with whole numbers.

1. dtorpuc

2. ums

3. lltimpuy

4. neiqotut

5. trabusdenh

6. derremnia

7. lttao

8. roacft

9. mnednui

10. dad

11. sivdiion

12. rwgbniroo

13. btcaruts

14. dddiiven

15. aedndd

16. svoirdi

Unscramble the following words which you would hear being used
in a math class

1. iuntngco

2. rpenetc

3. sste

4. raiontcf

5. ungeasmri

6. tttaisssic

7. megeoyrt

8. cidlasme

9. daniotid

10. atqeuonsi

11. citrem tesmys

12. trtonicabus

13. obarptlyiib

14. oarit

15. iodinsiv

16. ningourd

17. pproroniot

18. gciol

You may use any of the four operations in the puzzles
below, but you may use only the given number and you
must use it exactly the number of times allowed. Use
parentheses if necessary.

1.   Use 5-1s to make 2!

2.   Use 4-2s to make 10!

3.   Use 5-3s to make 3!

4.   Use 4-4s to make 20!

5.   Use 4-5s to make 80!

6.   Use 7-6s to make 5!

7.   Use 5-7s to make 49!

8.   Use 4-8s to make 1!

9.   Use 3-9s to make 3!

10.   Use 5-10s to make 11!

You may use any of the four operations in the puzzles
below, but you may use only the given number and you
must use it exactly the number of times allowed. Use
parentheses if necessary.

1. Use 4-2s to make 5!

2. Use 3-6s to make 30!

3. Use 4-9s to make 100!

4. Use 5-8s to make 0!

5. Use 6-1s to make 3!

6. Use 7-4s to make 9!

7. Use 5-10s to make 91!

8. Use 4-7s to make 8!

9. Use 5-5s to make 6!

10. Use 7-3s to make 30!

You may use any of the four operations in the puzzles
below, but you may use only the given numbers and you
must use them exactly the number of times allowed.
Use parentheses if necessary.

1. Use 2-3s and 2-2s to make 11!

2. Use 2-1s and 1-2 to make 3!

3. Use 2-5s and 3-7s to make 4!

4. Use 2-4s and 2-3s to make 9!

5. Use 3-4s and 1-1 to make 2!

6. Use 3-4s and 3-8s to make 2!

7. Use 2-5s and 2-2s to make 7!

8. Use 3-9s and 4-8s to make 1!

9. Use 4-3s and 3-10s to make 30!

10. Use 6-5s and 4-3s to make 2!

Place the numbers 0-9 in the following 10 boxes such
that no two consecutive numbers are placed next to
each other horizontally, vertically, or diagonally.

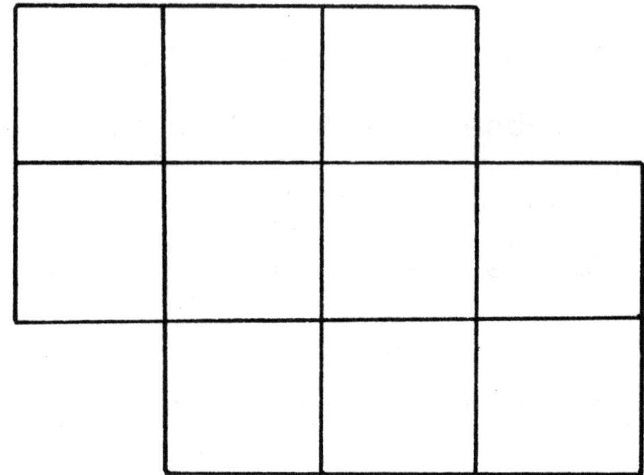

Place the numbers 1-9 in the following 9 boxes such that
no two consecutive numbers are placed next to each other
horizontally, vertically, or diagonally.

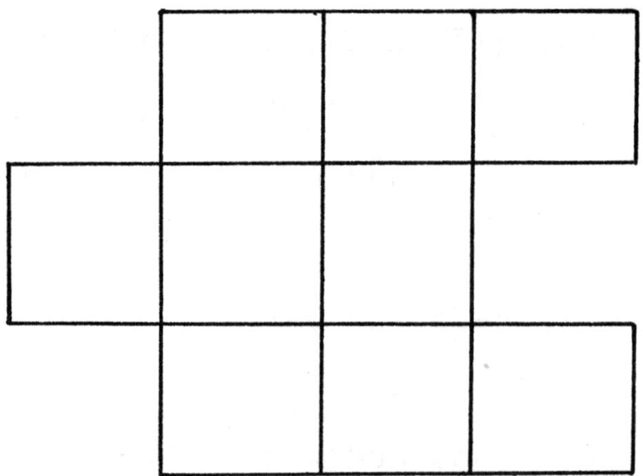

Place the numbers 1-10 in the following 10 boxes such
that no two consecutive numbers are placed next to
each other horizontally, vertically, or diagonally.

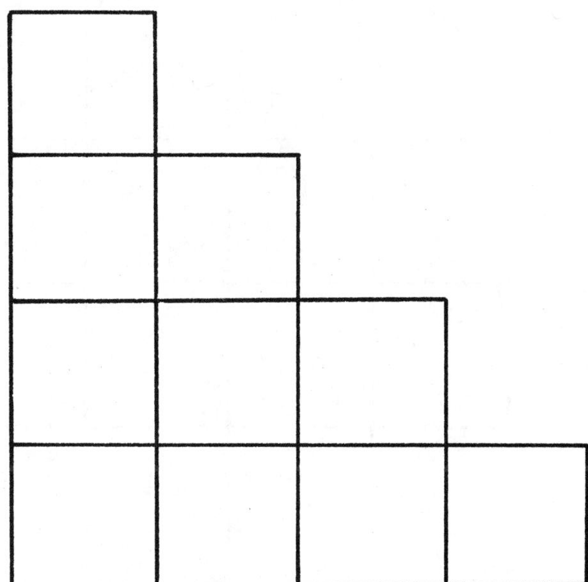

Place the numbers 1-8 in the following 8 boxes such
that no two consecutive numbers are placed next to
each other horizontally, vertically, or diagonally.

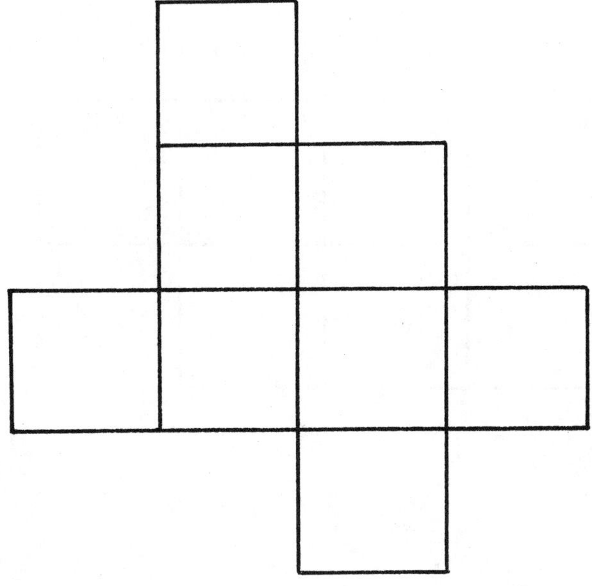

Place the numbers 1-10 in the following 10 boxes such that no two consecutive numbers are placed next to each other horizontally, vertically, or diagonally.

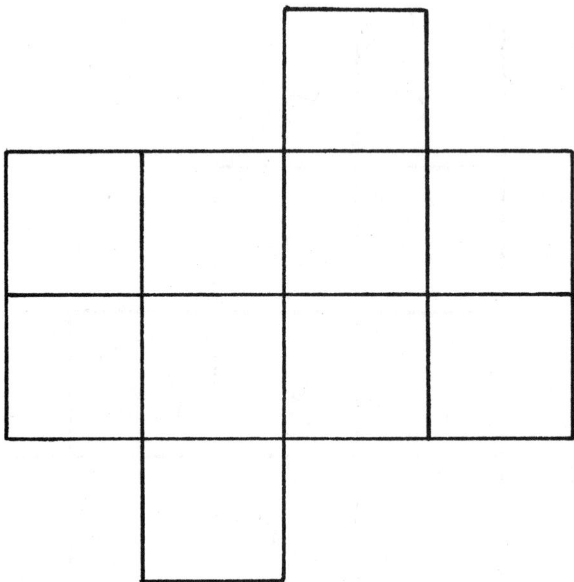

Place the numbers 1-10 in the following 10 boxes such that no two consecutive numbers are placed next to each other horizontally, vertically, or diagonally.

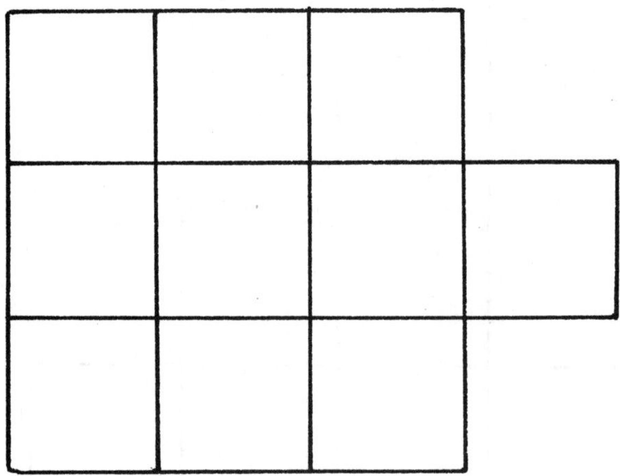

Look carefully at the problems below. You are to replace
the letters or symbols with numbers which make the problem
correct. In other words, you are to break the code used
to write each individual problem!

```
    A D A B              A B A B
      C B B            -   C C D
  +   C A A                B A C
    A B D A
```

```
      ! @ ! @                Y Z
  -   * * @ !            x      Z
      * * # *              X Y Z
```

```
        H A                    ? &
  x     H A              &⟌¢ &
        A E                    &
      H A                    $ &
      H E E                  $ &
```

You are to break the code used to write each individual
problem below. That is, you are to replace each letter
or symbol with a number which will make the problem
correct.

```
      E F G              A B C B
        G F           -  D E A C
  +   G E F              E A D D
    B D F G
```

```
      ? * %                V W
  x     $ !            x   G T
      ! $ *                I W
    $ ? *                V W
  $ % $ *                T V W
```

```
          Z Z                & @ &
  Y Z | Z X W         & # | ¢ & ¢ #
        Z W                ¢ #
        Z W                & ¢
        Z W                & #
                            ¢ #
                            ¢ #
```

Study the problems below. You are to replace the letters
or symbols with numbers which make the problem correct.
That is, you are to break the code used to write each
individual problem.


```
      A B C D                         R S T

        E B C                      -    R U
                                  ___________
          C D                        R R R
    + E A C C
    ___________
      C D B D
```


```
      L M N P                          ? : "

      M N M L                    ×      ° " "
                                  ___________
    +   M P N                          " " "

      L L P N M                      " " "
                             ______________________
                             :    ° ° "
                             _________________________
                             :    ° ° " " "
```


```
        !  *                            J I H
     _________                    F G )F H F I
     √ ! ? ?                           F G
                                      _____
                                       J F
                                        I
                                      _____
                                      J F I
                                      J F I
                                      =====
```

NUMBER PICTURES--Here are some hints: the loops on
nines are empty (9), but sixes will have a dot or number
inside their loop (6). Fives have straight spines (5),
but twos are curved (2).

Add the numbers
on the frog to
see how many
jumps he takes
per minute!

____

SUM A SUN POSIES:
Add the leaves and
petals to get the
surprising sum!

____

Total the numbers on each of the creatures below then
give a grand total for the page at the bottom. Here
are some hints: the loops on nines are empty (9), but
the loops on sixes have a dot or number inside them (6).
Fives have straight spines (5), but twos are curved (2).
Have fun, but Don't Get Bugged!!!!

Grand Total: _________

Total the numbers in each word, then total each line,
and then your total for the entire joke will be easy!
Here are some hints: the loops on nines are empty (9),
but the loops on sixes will have a dot in them (6).
Fives have straight spines (5), but twos are curved (2).
NOW!   START KNOCKING!!!

Knock Knock! _____

Who's There? _____

Euler! _____

Euler Who? _____

Eu-Rearn a Lot
in School!! _____

Page Total _____

Place the numbers given below in the criss-cross puzzle.
No number may be placed more than once. One number has
been located for you.

2 Digits	3 Digits	4 Digits	5 Digits	6 Digits	7 Digits
63	128	1734	13942	267843	6382195
67	276	2573	23562	295328	9284135
77	322	2722	42183	634815	
	395	3819	93458	987215	
	416	4341			
	538	5419			
	576	6795			
	621	8191			
	724	8526			
	816				
	827				

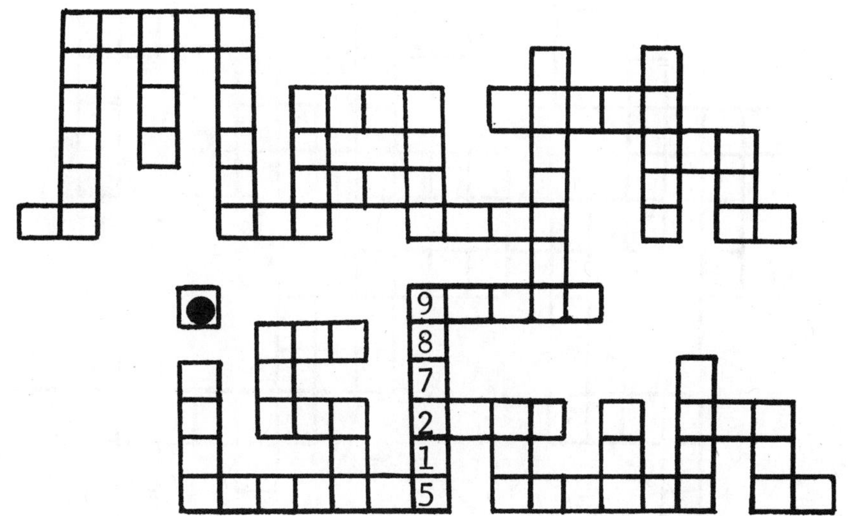

Place the numbers given below in the criss-cross
puzzle. No number may be placed more than once.
One number has been located for you.

<u>2 Digits</u>	<u>3 Digits</u>	<u>4 Digits</u>	<u>5 Digits</u>
17	315	2345	23451
38	317	2438	26928
43	328	3402	32459
59	413	3451	43076
77	475	3456	52401
92	514	3475	54923
	534	4027	57313
	718	5342	
	783	5436	
		5791	
		5976	
		9504	

Place the numbers given below in the criss-cross puzzle.
No number may be placed more than once. One number has
been located for you.

3 Digits	4 Digits	5 Digits	6 Digits
249	1036	23126	120313
283	1927	23165	129163
305	2928	28108	294067
431	3304	28718	321875
639	3314	42031	332056
642	3794	43236	510314
653	6023	51204	920831
705	6032	53175	931874
942	6431	62101	
	7563	63911	
	8632	65134	
	8724	71826	
		73175	

How many triangles do you see?

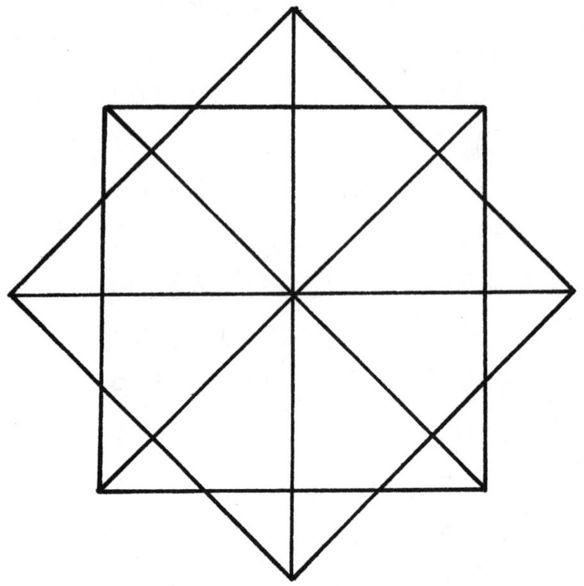

How many squares do you see?

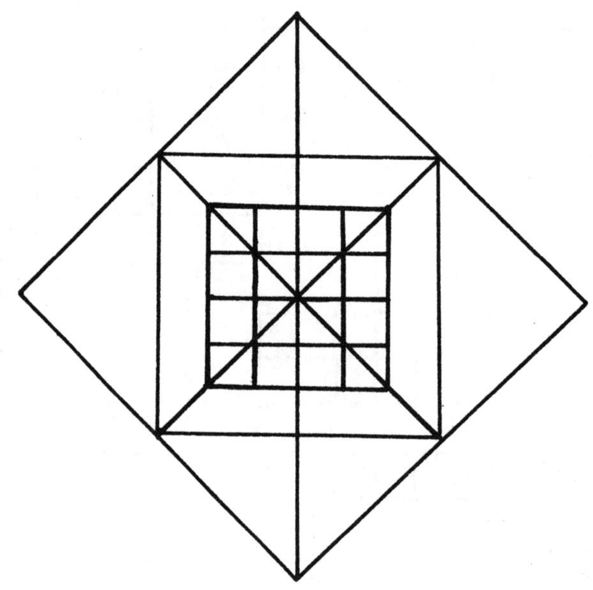

How many triangles do you see?

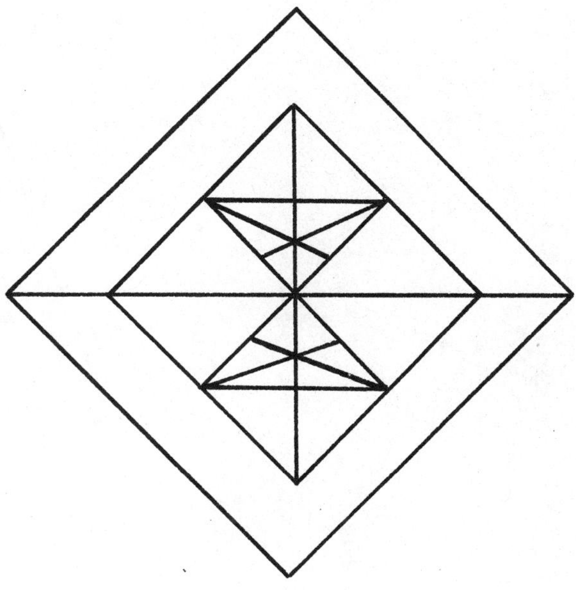

How many squares do you see?

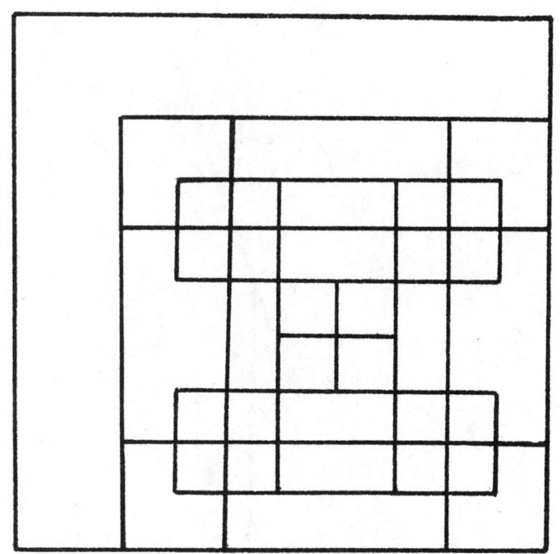

How many triangles do you see?

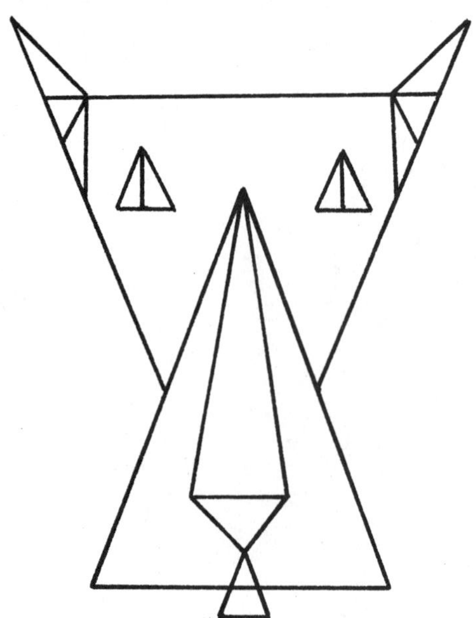

How many squares do you see?

In this number maze start at the top line and move to
the bottom making a total sum of 55. You can move
vertically and diagonally but not horizontally.

Example: Can you move through this maze making a
total sum of 15?

3	5	7	10	1	8
9	1	6	9	9	4
8	2	4	1	6	7
2	8	1	4	5	8

3	8	2	4	7	6	9	2	4	5
3	2	9	10	5	7	8	3	2	4
1	3	4	5	2	6	3	2	9	1
9	8	4	2	6	7	8	2	9	6
2	10	11	4	6	12	3	4	9	2
10	9	7	13	10	3	10	9	4	8
5	4	6	9	2	7	4	3	5	2
2	5	7	4	3	6	9	3	4	6

Can you move through this maze making a total
sum of 60?

5	4	9	2	6	8	3	4
5	6	7	8	9	5	8	9
8	9	5	4	10	12	3	5
11	14	7	6	8	9	4	6
3	8	15	16	9	2	17	10
9	3	10	4	8	2	7	6
6	7	3	8	4	9	2	8
5	8	4	7	6	3	5	7
4	6	7	9	3	5	6	4

In this number maze start at the top line and move
to the bottom making a total sum of 17. You can
move vertically and diagonally but not horizontally.

Example: Can you move through this maze making a
           total sum of 15?

3	5	7	10	1	8
9	1	6	9	9	4
8	2	4	1	6	7
2	8	1	4	5	8

3	5	2	8	9	0	7	6
3	6	8	2	3	5	1	4
4	9	2	1	7	6	3	5
1	4	7	6	9	6	4	2
8	6	4	2	6	9	7	0
9	3	3	4	6	7	9	2

Can you move through this maze making a total
sum of 50?

5	9	6	2	6	3	4	5
8	7	5	4	5	2	3	1
2	4	3	1	8	5	6	7
3	5	2	9	7	4	9	6
9	7	6	8	5	3	1	4
8	5	7	4	2	4	3	5
2	4	0	7	6	5	4	1
1	2	7	6	3	2	4	3
9	2	8	7	6	5	9	8
9	4	3	8	9	6	7	2

In this number maze start at the top line and move
to the bottom making a total sum of 28. You can
move vertically and diagonally but not horizontally.

Example: Can you move through this maze making a
           total sum of 15?

3	5	7	10	1	8
9	1	6	9	9	4
8	2	4	1	6	7
2	8	1	4	5	8

3	6	9	7	8	10	2	4
2	1	6	3	4	9	5	7
15	8	7	14	2	11	10	6
4	5	9	3	1	17	12	1
4	5	7	4	3	8	11	19
2	11	10	8	10	2	7	8
4	3	5	2	1	4	5	4
3	2	9	8	7	8	9	11
2	1	6	5	4	3	2	6

Can you move through this maze making a total
sum of 31?

4	3	2	10	12	9	1	7	5	2	5
2	1	4	9	3	1	6	9	12	11	7
15	12	14	1	10	12	8	3	11	13	9
8	7	6	9	12	14	4	7	3	8	9
3	9	12	10	7	12	14	8	7	12	9
1	3	4	5	9	7	4	3	9	10	3
8	6	10	7	12	4	5	10	3	9	3
4	3	5	8	9	1	11	5	11	14	4

Look carefully in the picture below and see if you can
find the four letters that are in the word 'math'. Here
are some hints: the letters are randomly placed (that
is, they do not spell out math), the letters are all
approximately the same size, and they are written in
block form like the ones just below.

MATH

Now, let's see if you can find all four of the letters!!

Somewhere in the picture below there is a toothbrush just like the one drawn at the right- except the one you are to find is bigger! See if you can find it!!!

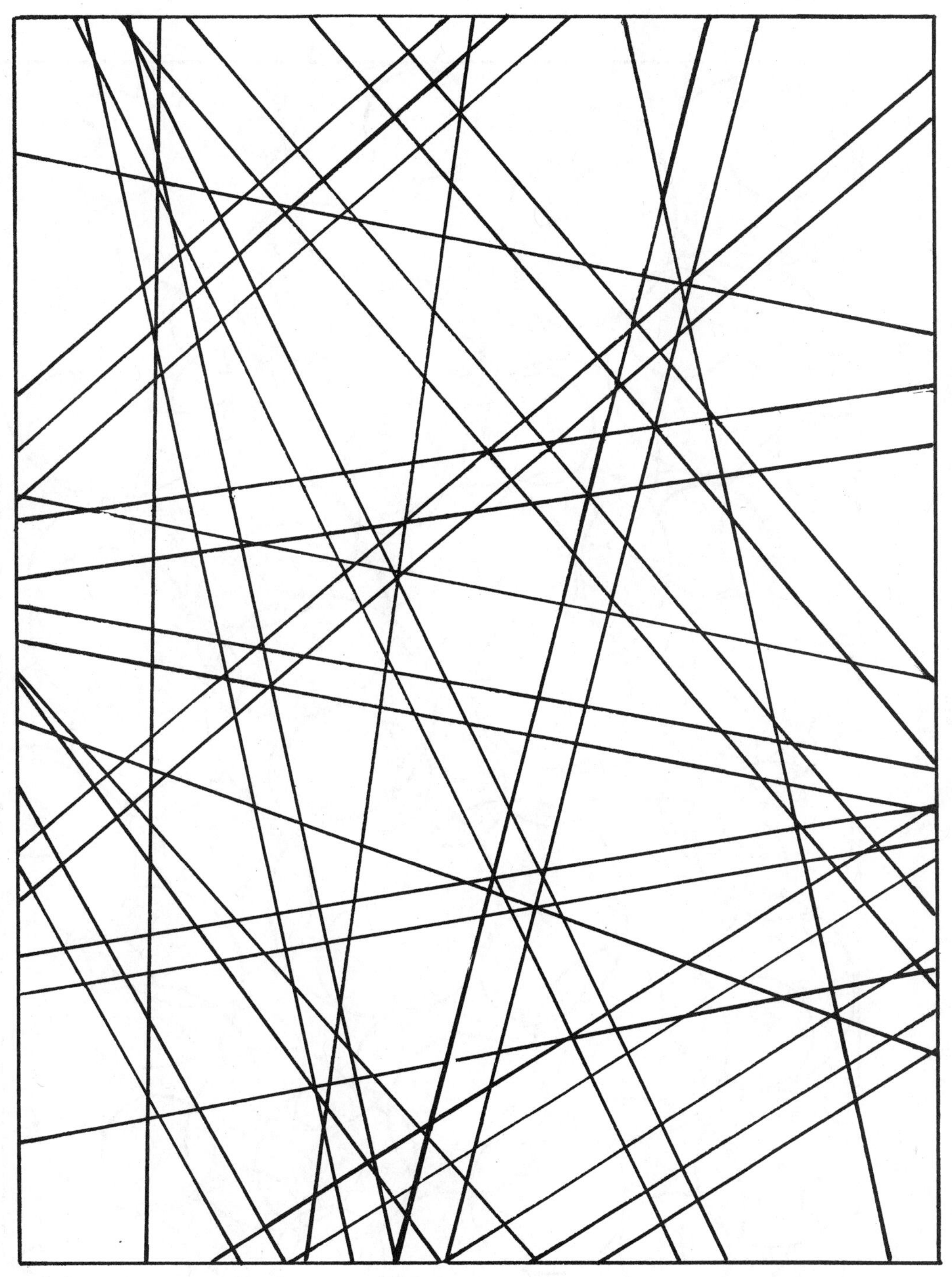

In the picture below you will find a bear just
like the one drawn to the right of the directions
only it will be a <u>different size</u>. Time yourself
and see how long it takes you to find the bear!!!

54

The dots in the picture below represent horses.
Draw 6 lines (border to border) so that each
horse is fenced off by itself.

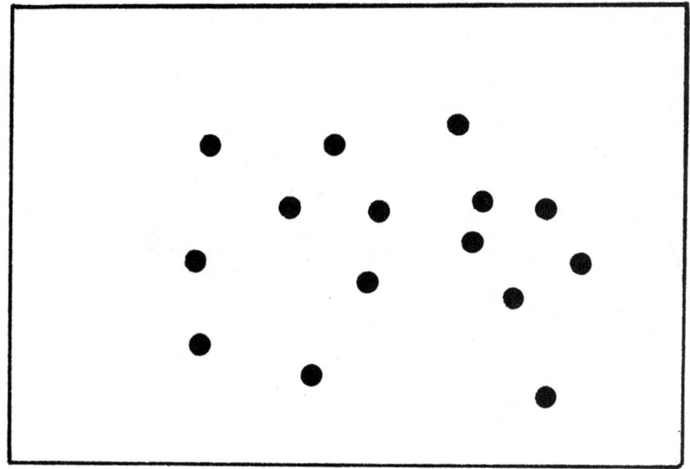

Can you draw 5 lines to fence these horses in?

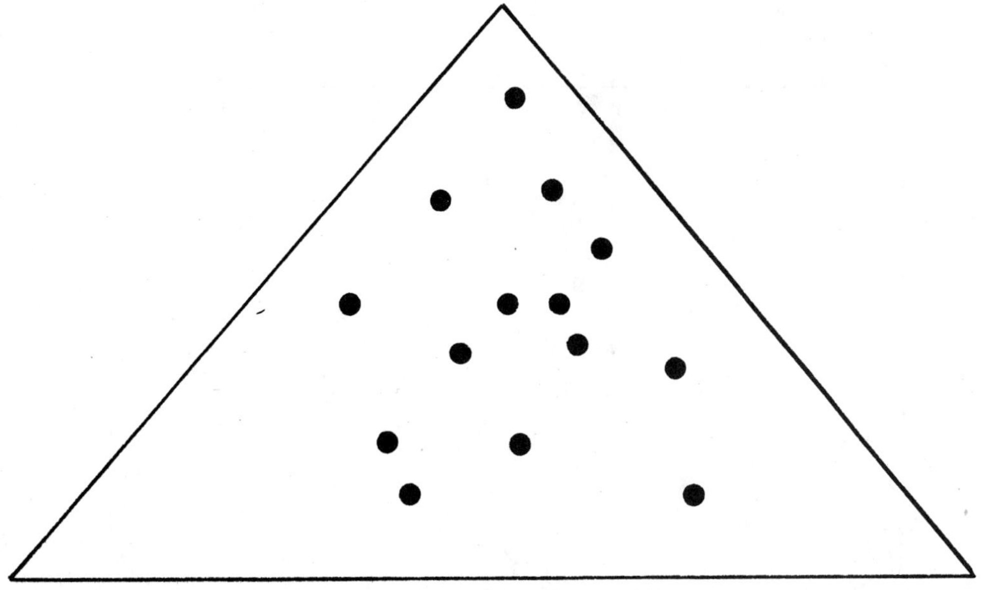

The dots in the picture below represent horses.
Draw 5 lines (border to border) so that each
horse is fenced off by itself.

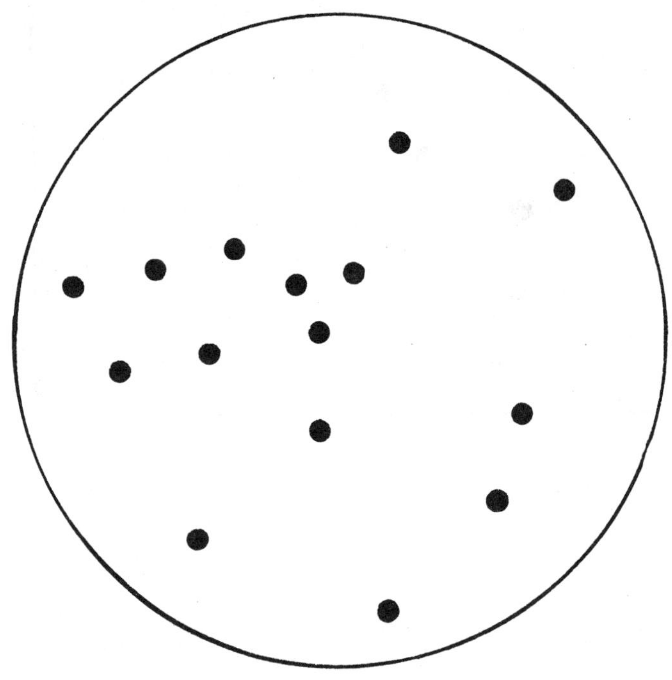

Can you draw 5 lines to fence these horses in?

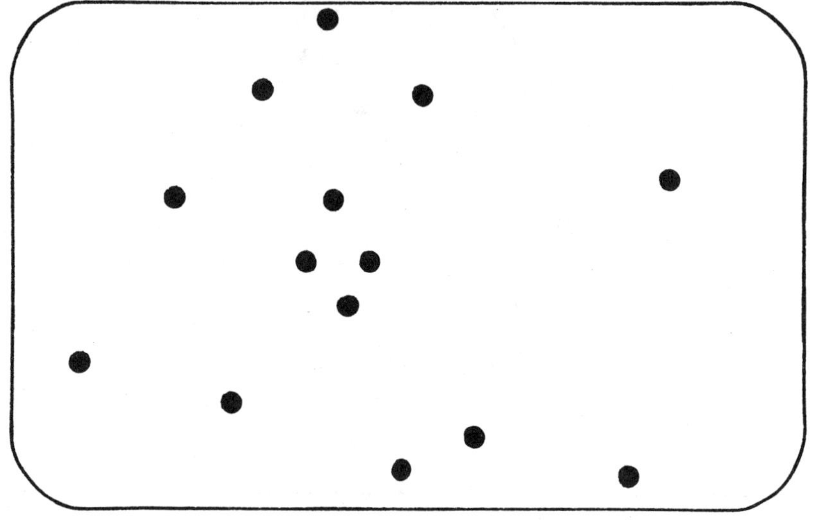

The dots in the picture below represent horses.
Draw 5 lines (border to border) so that each
horse is fenced off by itself.

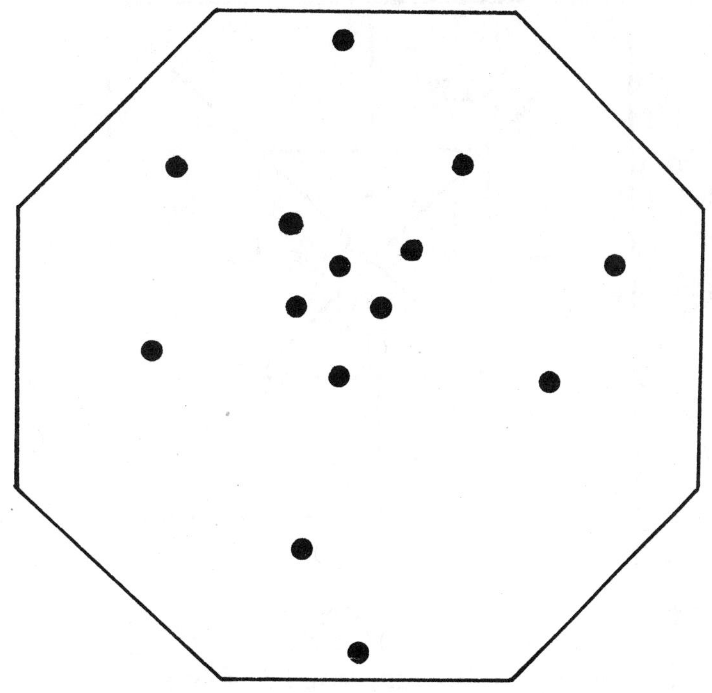

Can you draw 5 lines to fence these horses in?

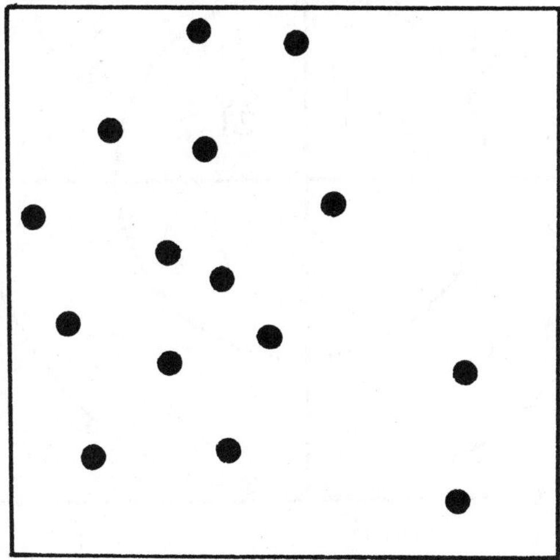

The picture below represents a target. Can you
make 5 shots at the target making a total score of 102?
(No number was used twice and each shot hit the target.)

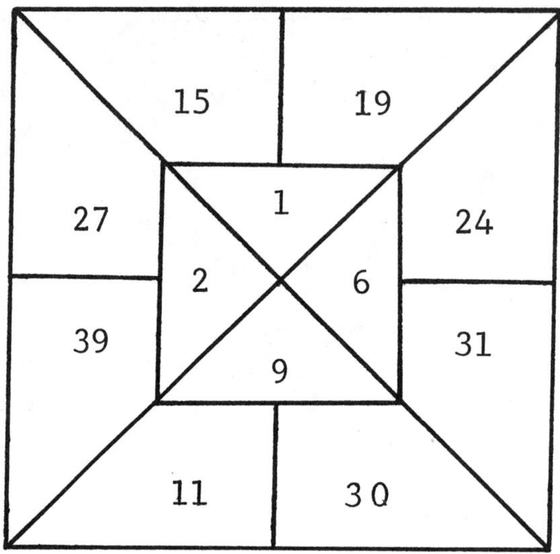

Can you find what 5 shots would give you a total of 85?

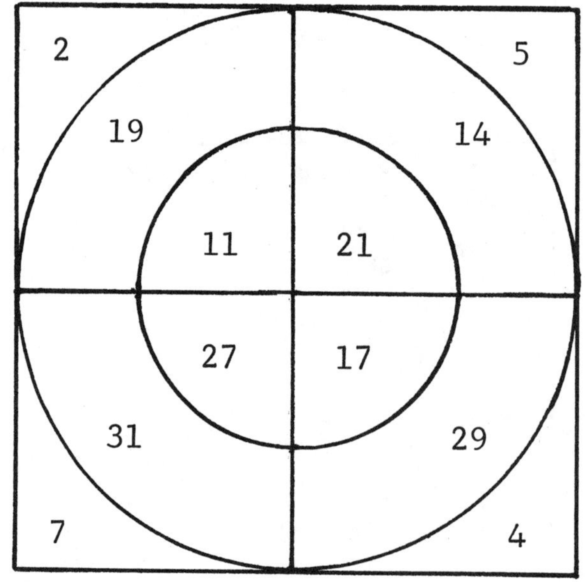

The picture below represents a target. Can you make 4
shots at the target making a total score of 60?
(No number was used twice and each shot hit the target.)

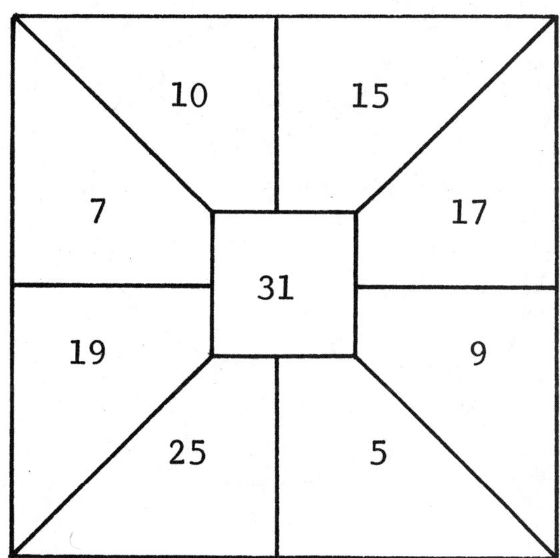

Can you find what 4 shots would give you a total of 84?

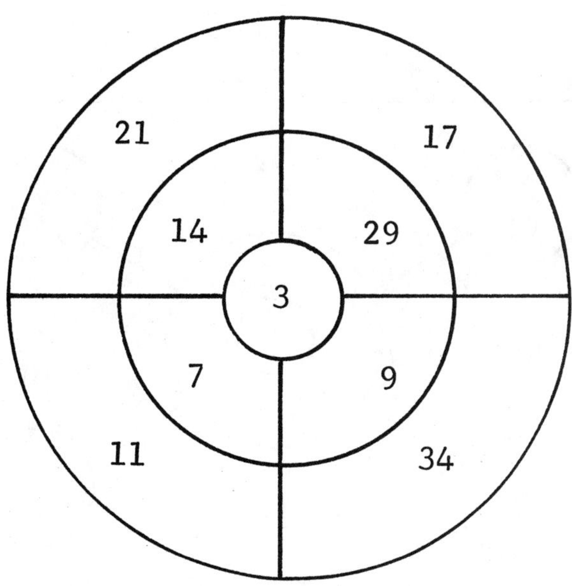

The picture below represents a target. Can you make
5 shots at the target making a total score of 116?
(No number was used twice and each shot hit the target.)

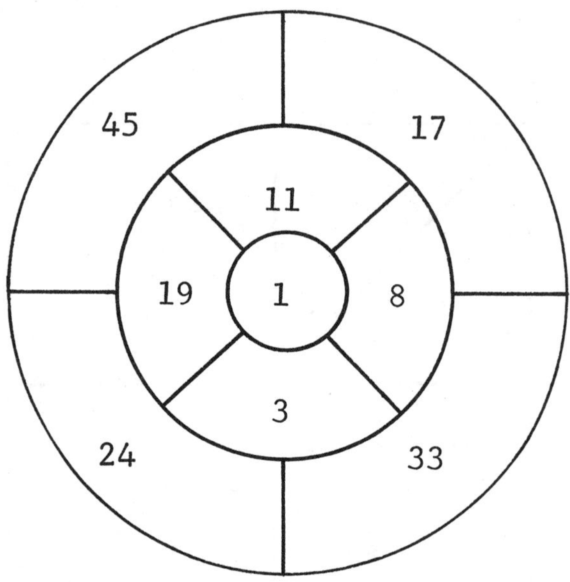

Can you find what 5 shots would give you a total of 71?

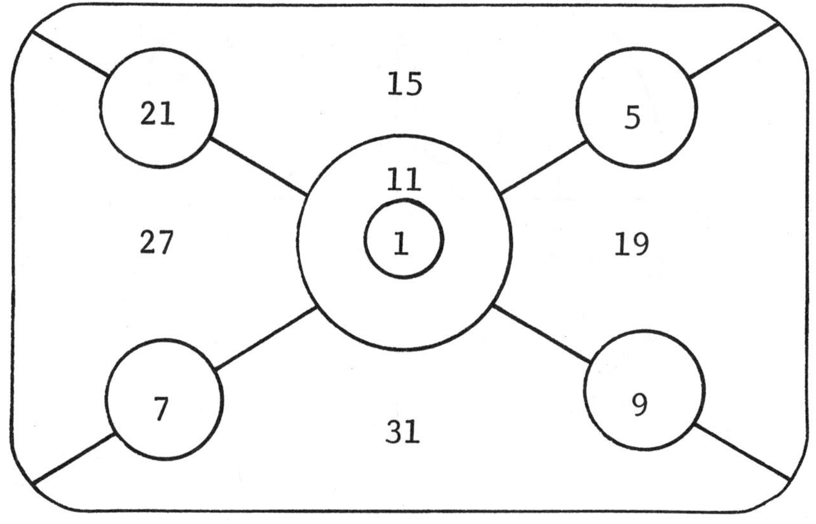

Page 1 - 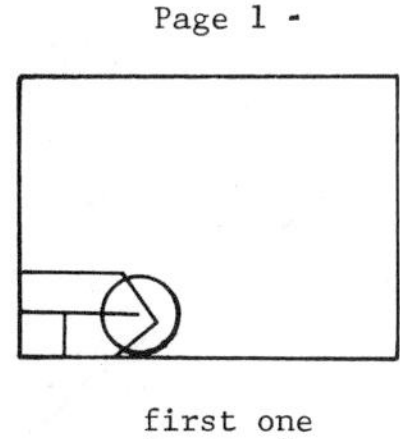

first one
in row 2

Page 2 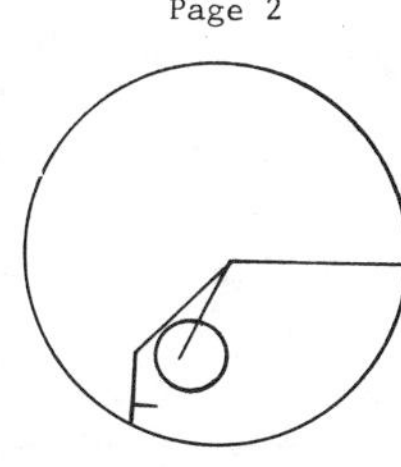

second one
in row 1

Page 3 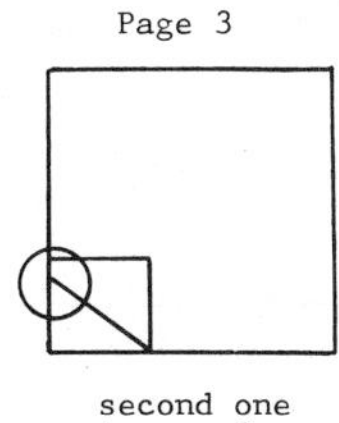

second one
in row 3

1A-3A

1. 720, 5040, 40320
   Pattern: Ax2=B, Bx3=C, Cx4=D, ...

2. 16, 9, 14
   Pattern: A+5=B, B-7=C, C+5=D, D-7=E,...

3. 16, 36, 20
   Pattern: 1st, 3rd, 5th, ... are multiples of 4
            2nd, 4th, 6th, ... are multiples of 9

4. 17, 20, 21
   Pattern: A+1=B, B+2=C, C+3=D, D+1=E, E+2=F, F+3=G, ...

5. 31, 33, 41
   Pattern: A+1=B, B+2=C, C+5=D, D+1=E, E+2=F, F+6=G,
            G+1=H, H+2=J, J+7=K, K+1=L, L+2=M, M+8=N, ...

6. 36, 49, 64
   Pattern: 1x1, 2x2, 3x3, 4x4, 5x5, 6x6, ...

7. 216, 343, 512
   Pattern: 1x1x1, 2x2x2, 3x3x3, 4x4x4, 5x5x5, 6x6x6, ...

8. 30, 6, 42
   Pattern: 1st, 3rd, 5th,... count by 1s--1, 2, 3, 4, ...
            2nd+4=4th, 4th+6=6th, 6th+8=8th, 8th+10=10th,...

9. 32, 5, 37
   Pattern: 2nd, 4th, 6th,... obtained by adding digits of
            the 1st, 3rd, 5th,...
            3rd=1st+2nd, 5th=3rd+4th, 7th=5th+6th,...

10. 25, 10, 15
    Pattern: 2nd, 4th, 6th,... obtained by multiplying
             digits of the 1st, 3rd, 5th,...
             2nd+5=3rd, 4th+5=5th, 6th+5=7th, 8th+5=9th,...

4A

1. 77, 100, 129
   Pattern: A+2=B, B+3=C, C+5=D, D+7=E, E+11=F,...
            To each number you add the next successive prime.

2. 80, 82, 241
   Pattern: A+1=B, B+2=C, C+B+A=D, D+1=E, E+2=F, F+E+D=G,...

3. 22, 23, 24
   Pattern: whole numbers in sequence beginning with the
            letter "t"

4. 12, 13, 20
   Pattern: two, three, four, five, six, seven, eight, eleven,
            nine, nineteen, ten, twelve, thirteen, twenty

5. 0, 6, 12
   Pattern: A, B, &C are multiples of 2, D, E, &F are
            multiples of 3, then multiples of 4, ...

6. 10, 5, 1
   Pattern: A-10=B, B-9=C, C-8=D, D-7=E, E-6=F, ...

7. 103, 104, 110
   Pattern: counting numbers from 33_{five} to 110_{five}

8. O, N, D
   Pattern: first letter of the twelve months

9. F, U, G
   Pattern: 1st, 3rd, 5th, ... alphabet in sequence
            2nd, 4th, 6th, ... alphabet backwards

10. E, N, D
    Pattern: 1st, 3rd, 5th, ... spell sixteen
             2nd, 4th, 6th, ... spell hundred

5A

1. 17, 19, 23
   Pattern: prime numbers

2. 514800, 25225200, 1614413800
   Pattern: Ax1x1=B, Bx2x2=C, Cx3x3=D, Dx4x4=E, ...

3. 69, 138, 141
   Pattern: A+3=B, Bx2=C, C+3=D, Dx2=E, E+3=F, Fx2=G, ...

4. 61, 36, 85
   Pattern: 1st, 3rd, 5th, ... = 1^2, 2^2, 3^2, ...
            2nd=1st+3rd, 4th=3rd+5th, 6th=5th+7th, ...

5. 216, 432, 1296
   Pattern: Ax2=B, Bx3=C, Cx2=D, Dx3=E, ...

6. $16/243$, $32/729$, $64/2187$
   Pattern: Ax2/3=B, Bx2/3=C, Cx2/3=D, ...

7. $2 5/6$, $3 1/6$, $3 1/2$
   Pattern: A+1/3=B, B+1/3=C, C+1/3=D, D+1/3=E, ...

8. $1/720$, $1/5040$, $1/40320$
   Pattern: Ax1/2=B, Bx1/3=C, Cx1/4=D, Dx1/5=E, ...

9. 30, $3 3/4$, 38
   Pattern: 1st/3=2nd, 1st+3=3rd, 3rd/4=4th, 3rd+4=5th,
            5th/5=6th, 5th+5=7th, 7th/6=8th, 7th+6=9th, ...

10. .100001, .1000001, .10000001
    Pattern: one zero, two zeros, three zeros, four zeros,...

6A

40	5	30
15	25	35
20	45	10

31	3	5	25
9	21	19	15
17	13	11	23
7	27	29	1

7A

80	10	15	65
25	55	50	40
45	35	30	60
20	70	75	5

34	48	2	16	30
46	10	14	28	32
8	12	26	40	44
20	24	38	42	6
22	36	50	4	18

8A

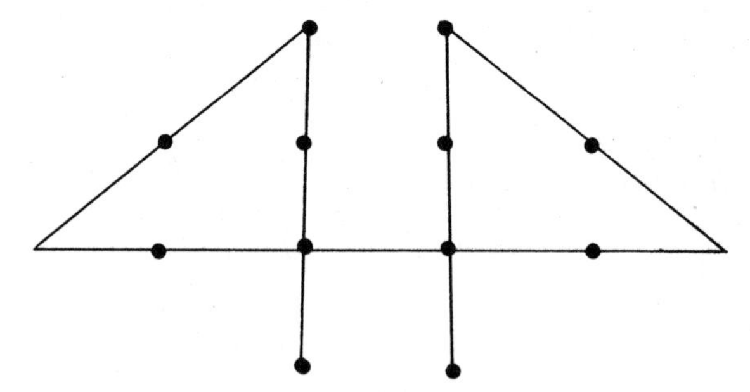

17	24	1	8	15
23	5	7	14	16
4	6	13	20	22
10	12	19	21	3
11	18	25	2	9

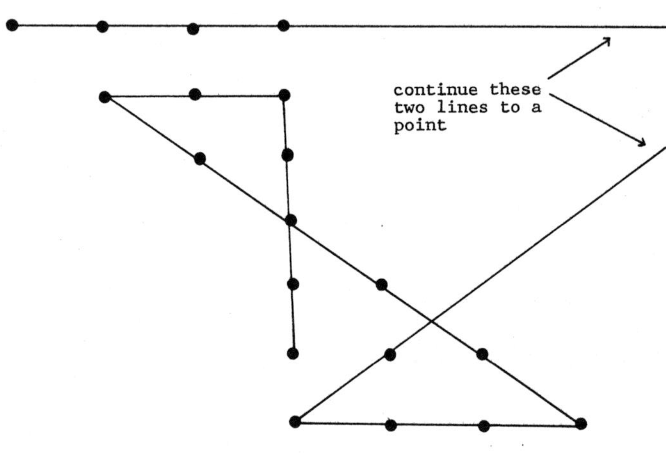

10A

64	2	3	61	60	6	7	57
9	55	54	12	13	51	50	16
17	47	46	20	21	43	42	24
40	26	27	37	36	30	31	33
32	34	35	29	28	38	39	25
41	23	22	44	45	19	18	48
49	15	14	52	53	11	10	56
8	58	59	5	4	62	63	1

9A

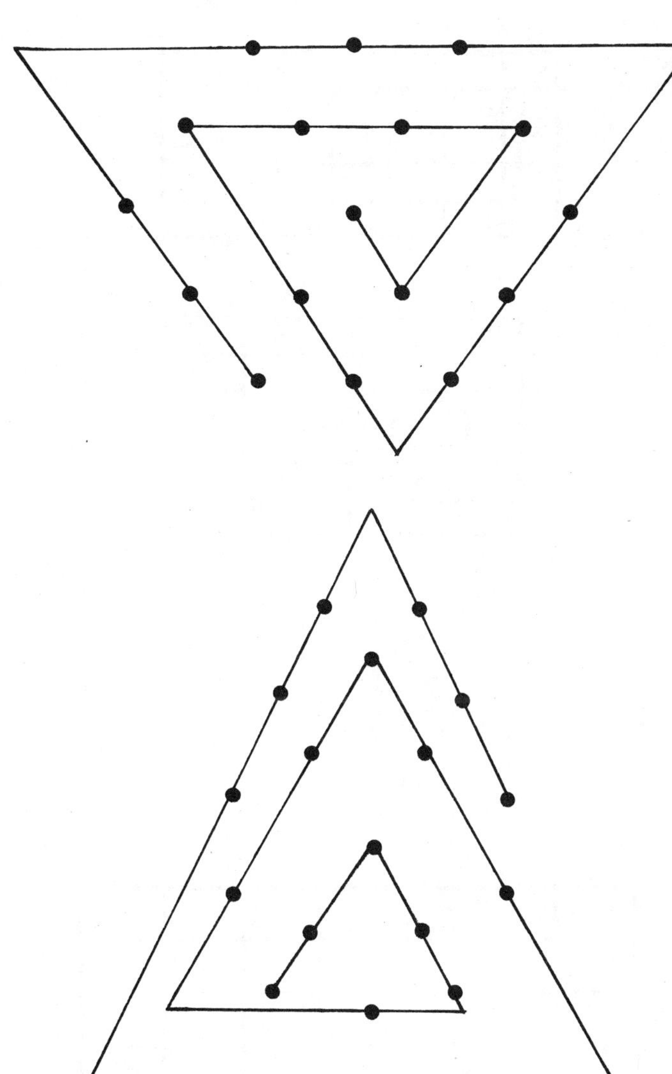

11A

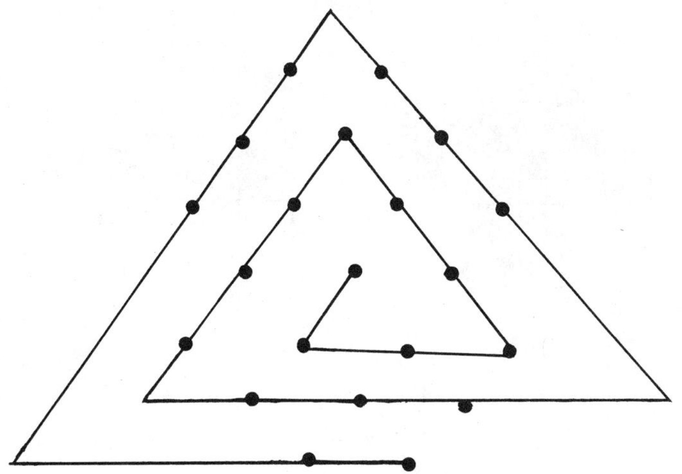

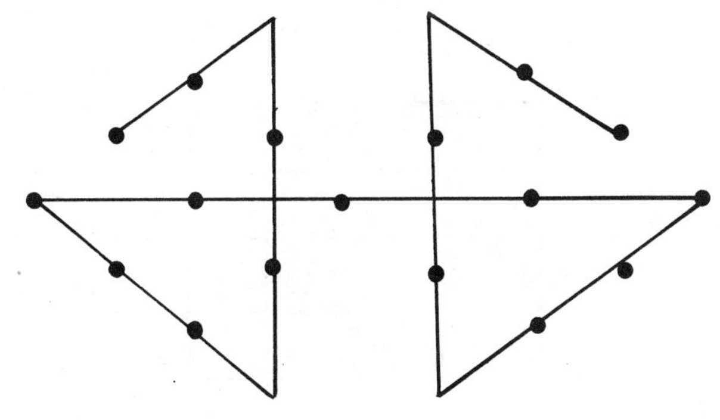

12A

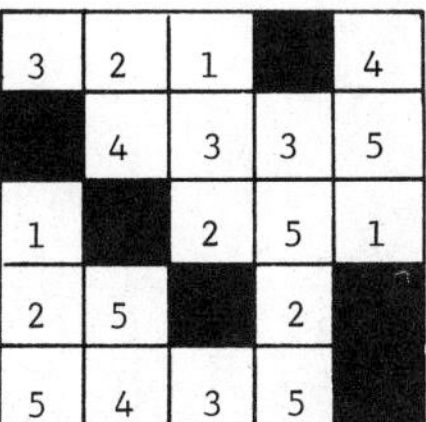

3	2	1	■	4
■	4	3	3	5
1	■	2	5	1
2	5	■	2	■
5	4	3	5	■

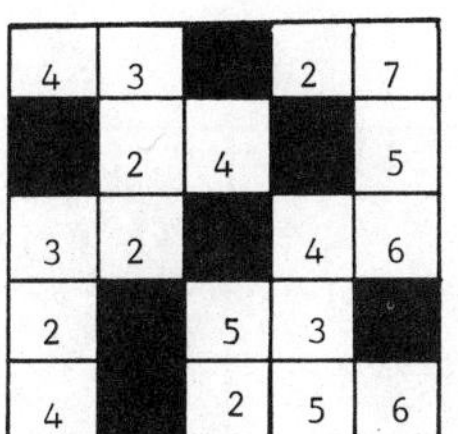

4	3	■	2	7
■	2	4	■	5
3	2	■	4	6
2	■	5	3	■
4	■	2	5	6

13A

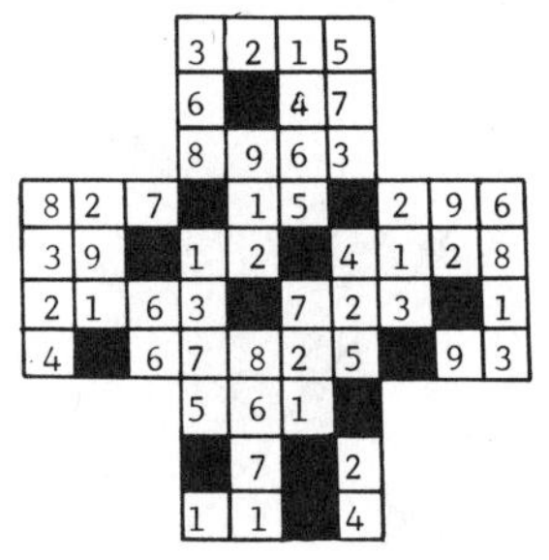

14A

15A

16A

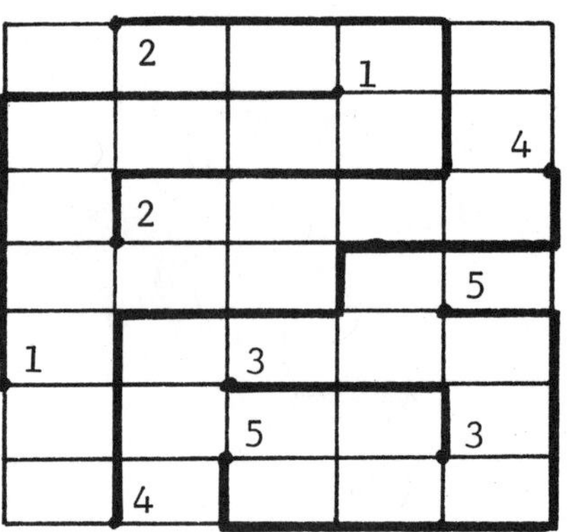

17A

18A

19A

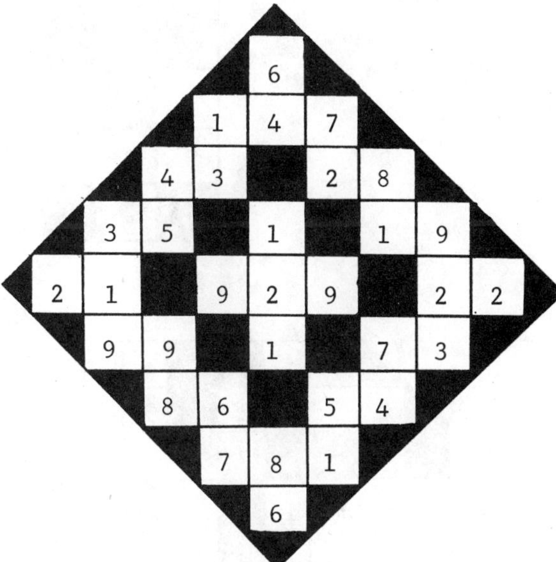

20A

Answers may vary slightly.

Grid 1:

2	■	9	1	9	■	4	5
7	3	9	■	3	6	■	1
1	1	■			2	8	1
					■	6	■
					9	■	2
					9	3	2
					■	4	■
					3	■	4
					9	9	9
					■	5	■

Grid 2:

■	1	1	■	■	9		
2	5	8	1	■	9		
8	■	■	7	3	9		
		1	■	2	■		
		1	■	1	6		
		7	8	■	3		
		■	6	4	■		
		1	■	2	8		
		6	9	■	8		
■	2	1	■	7	■	2	9
5	7	■	1	1	1	■	6
3	■	4	6	■	5	9	8

21A

1. 42 - 4 + 1 - 24 = 15

2. 6 + 42 - 32 = 16

3. 9 - 6 + 32 - 21 = 14

4. 2 + 4 - 3 + 12 - 3 = 12

5. 8 - 6 + 24 - 4 + 2 = 24

6. 9 - 3 + 6 - 2 + 31 = 41

7. 1 + 21 - 2 - 12 = 8

8. 3 + 21 + 3 - 21 = 6

22A

1. (3 + 21) ÷ (12 ÷ 3) = 6

2. (12 + 33) ÷ (2 + 1) = 15

3. 6 - 5 + 4 - (3 + 2) = 0

4. 12 - 64 ÷ 32 = 10

5. $\left[123 - (4 + 5)\right] ÷ 6$ = 19

6. (424 - 4) ÷ 28 = 15

7. 65 - 44 ÷ (5 + 6) = 61

8. (23 - 4 - 4) ÷ (3 + 2) = 3

23A

1. 3 ÷ (2 + 1) X 2 X 2 = 4

2. 42 ÷ (4 + 2) + 2 = 9

3. 24 X 12 ÷ 6 ÷ 3 - 2 - 1 = 13

4. 16 ÷ 8 + 42 - 12 = 32

5. (4 + 2 + 24) ÷ (2 + 4) = 5

6. (24 + 12 + 6) - 42 ÷ 2 = 21

7. (16 + 84) X 2 ÷ 4 = 50

8. 24 X 12 - (63 X 2 X 2) = 36

24A

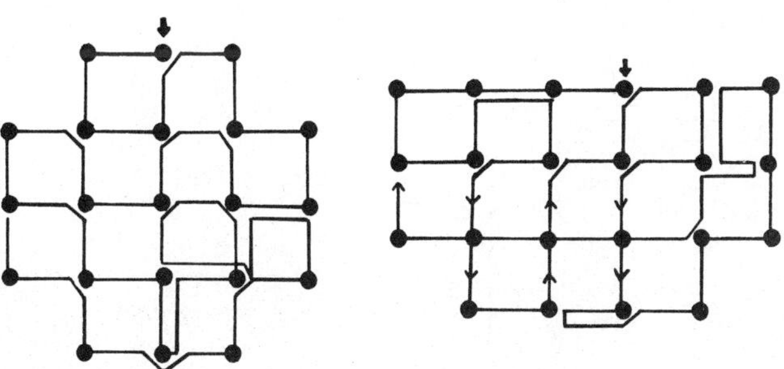

25A

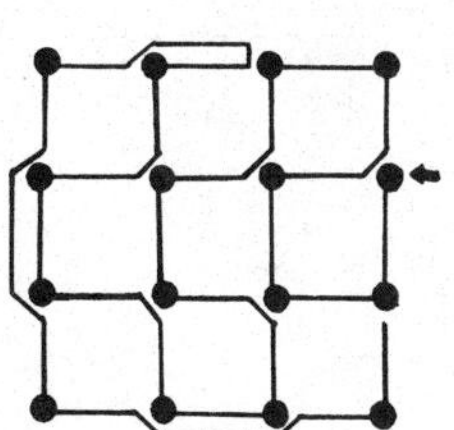
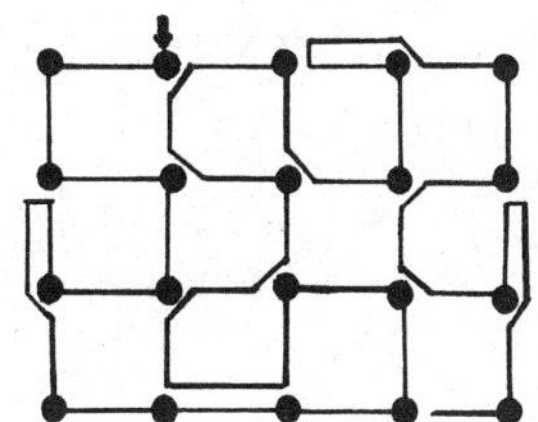

26A

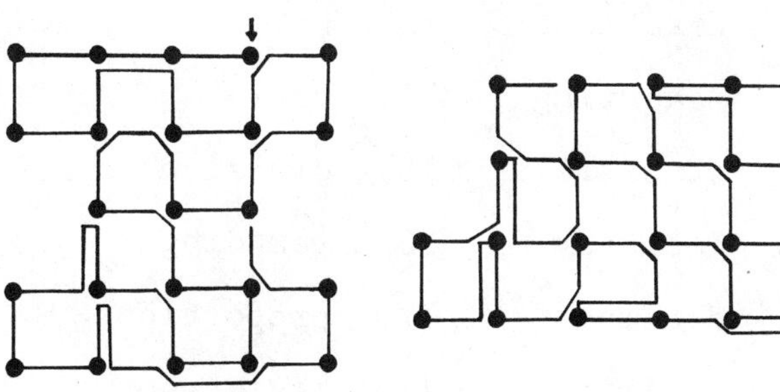

27A

1.	zero	11.	sixty
2.	twenty-one	12.	eleven
3.	thirty	13.	forty
4.	fifty-two	14.	nineteen
5.	eighty	15.	twenty-two
6.	fifty	16.	forty-four
7.	eight	17.	ninety-one
8.	ninety	18.	seven
9.	hundred	19.	seventy
10.	twelve		

28A

1.	product	9.	minuend
2.	sum	10.	add
3.	multiply	11.	division
4.	quotient	12.	borrowing
5.	subtrahend	13.	subtract
6.	remainder	14.	dividend
7.	total	15.	addend
8.	factor	16.	divisor

29A

1.	counting	10.	equations
2.	percent	11.	metric system
3.	sets	12.	subtraction
4.	fraction	13.	probability
5.	measuring	14.	ratio
6.	statistics	15.	division
7.	geometry	16.	rounding
8.	decimals	17.	proportion
9.	addition	18.	logic

30A

1. $1^{11}/11$ or $1^{11} + 1^1 = 2$

2. $(22 - 2) \div 2 = 10$

3. $33 - 3^3 - 3$ or $3 + 3 + 3 - 3 - 3 = 3$

4. $4 \times 4^4/4 = 20$

5. $5 \times 5 + 55 = 80$

6. $(6 \times 6 - {}^6/6) \div 6^6/6 = 5$

7. $7(7 + 7) - 7 \times 7 = 49$

8. $8^8/8 - 8 = 1$

9. $(9 \times \sqrt{9}) \div 9 = 3$

10. $10^{10}/10 \times {}^{10}/10 = 11$

31A

1. $2 + 2^2/2 = 5$	1. $33 - 22 = 11$ or $2 \times 3 + 2 + 3 = 11$
2. $6 \times 6 - 6 = 30$	2. $2^1/1 = 3$
3. $99^9/9 = 100$	3. $5 \times 5 - (7 + 7 + 7) = 4$
4. $(88 - 88) \div 8$ or $(^8/8 - {}^8/8) \div 8 = 0$	4. $43 - 34 = 9$
5. $1^1/1 + 1 + 1 - 1$ or $1^{11}/11 + 1 = 3$	5. $4 \times 4 - 14 = 2$
6. $44^4/4 \div 4^4/4$ or $^{44}/4 - {}^4/4 - {}^4/4 = 9$	6. $^{48}/4 - 8^8/4 = 2$
7. $10 \times 10 - 10 + {}^{10}/10 = 91$	7. $2^5 - 5^2 = 7$
8. $(7 \times 7 + 7) \div 7 = 8$	8. $(89 + 8 - 9 \times 9) \div (8 + 8) = 1$
9. $^{55}/55 + 5 = 6$	9. $3(^{10^3}/10) - 10 \times 3^3 = 30$
10. $^{333}/3 - 3 \times 3^3 = 30$	10. $355 - (53 \times 5) - (55 + 33) = 2$
32A	33A

0 3 1
8 6 9 5
4 2 7

2 7 4
8 5 9
3 1 6

34A

10
5 3 8 2
7 1 6 4
9

5 7 2
3 10 4 9
1 8 6

36A

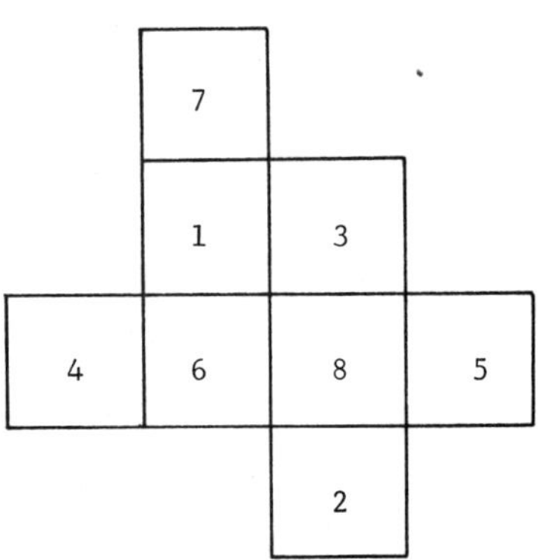

35A

Answers may vary.

1. A = 3   2. A = 1   3. ! = 2
    B = 5   B = 5   @ = 3
    C = 1   C = 9   * = 1
    D = 2   D = 6   # = 9

4. X = 1   5. H = 1   6. ? = 1
    Y = 2   A = 2   & = 5
    Z = 5   E = 4   ¢ = 7
                             $ = 2

37A

Answers may vary.

1. B = 1	2. A = 3	3. ? = 1
D = 0	B = 5	* = 0
E = 3	C = 4	% = 5
F = 5	D = 1	$ = 2
G = 6	E = 2	! = 4

4. V = 2	5. W = 4	6. & = 2
W = 5	X = 6	# = 0
G = 1	Y = 1	¢ = 4
T = 3	Z = 2	@ = 1
I = 7		

Answers may vary.

1. A = 1	2. R = 4	3. L = 1
B = 0	S = 8	M = 8
C = 3	T = 5	N = 5
D = 4	U = 1	P = 2
E = 2		

4. ? = 3	5. ! = 1	6. F = 2
: = 1	? = 4	G = 4
" = 0	* = 2	H = 5
° = 5		I = 0
		J = 1

40A-42A

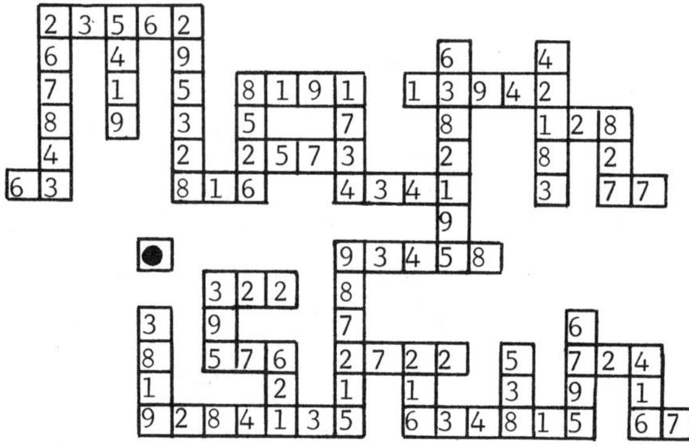

43A

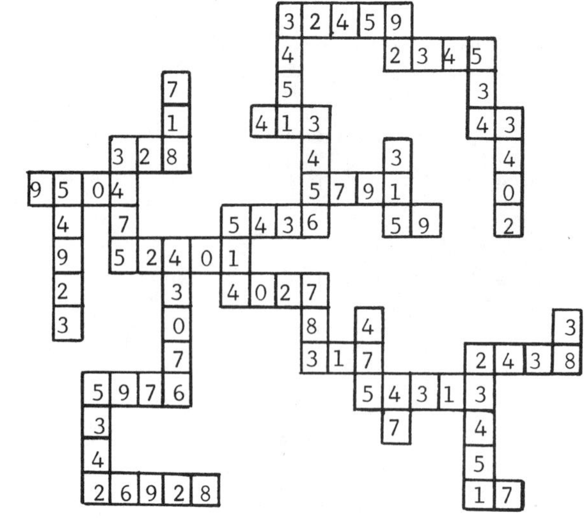

44A

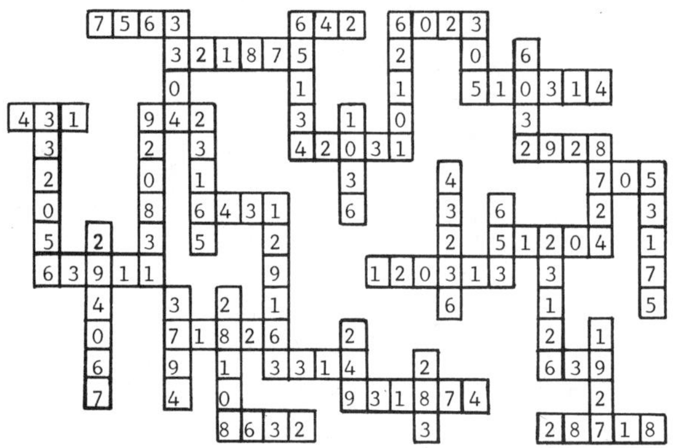

45A

46A-48A

3	8	2	4	7	6	9	2	4	5
3	2	9	10	5	7	8	3	2	4
1	3	4	5	2	6	3	2	9	1
9	8	4	2	6	7	8	2	9	6
2	10	11	4	6	12	3	4	9	2
10	9	7	1-3	10	3	10	9	4	8
5	4	6	9	2	7	4	3	5	2
2	5	7	4	3	6	9	3	4	6

5	4	9	2	6	8	3	4
5	6	7	8	9	5	8	9
8	9	5	4	10	12	3	5
11	14	7	6	8	9	4	6
3	8	15	16	9	2	17	10
9	3	10	4	8	2	7	6
6	7	3	8	4	9	2	8
5	8	4	7	6	3	5	7
4	6	7	9	3	5	6	4

49A

3	5	2	8	9	0	7	6
3	6	8	2	3	5	1	4
4	9	2	1	7	6	3	5
1	4	7	6	9	6	4	2
8	6	4	2	6	9	7	0
9	3	3	4	6	7	9	2

5	9	6	2	6	3	4	5
8	7	5	4	5	2	3	1
2	4	3	1	8	5	6	7
3	5	2	9	7	4	9	6
9	7	6	8	5	3	1	4
8	5	7	4	2	4	3	5
2	4	0	7	6	5	4	1
1	2	7	6	3	2	4	3
9	2	8	7	6	5	9	8
9	4	3	8	9	6	7	2

50A

3	6	9	7	8	10	2	4
2	1	6	3	4	9	5	7
15	8	7	14	2	11	10	6
4	5	9	3	1	17	12	1
4	5	7	4	3	8	11	19
2	11	10	8	10	2	7	8
4	3	5	2	1	4	5	4
3	2	9	8	7	8	9	11
2	1	6	5	4	3	2	6

4	3	2	10	12	9	1	7	5	2	5
2	1	4	9	3	1	6	9	12	11	7
15	12	14	1	10	12	8	3	11	13	9
8	7	6	9	12	14	4	7	3	8	9
3	9	12	10	7	12	14	8	7	12	•9
1	3	4	5	9	7	4	3	9	10	3
8	6	10	7	12	4	5	10	3	9	3
4	3	5	8	9	1	11	5	11	14	4

51A

52A

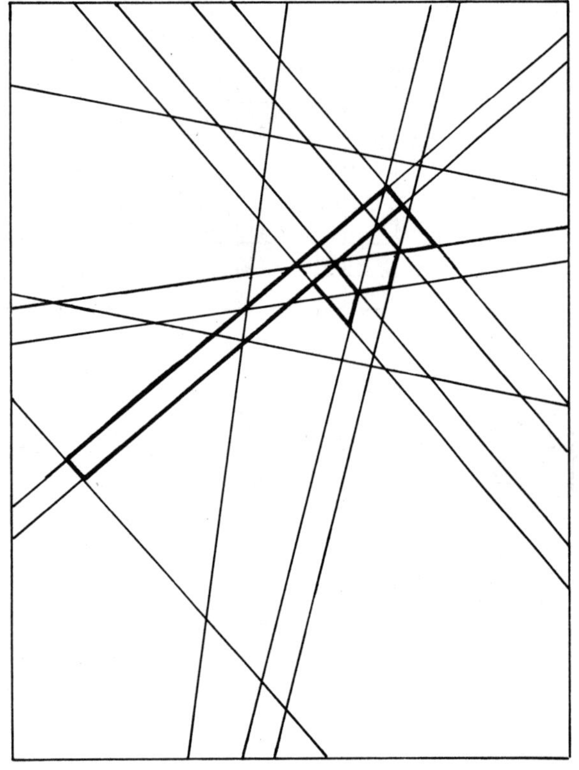

53A

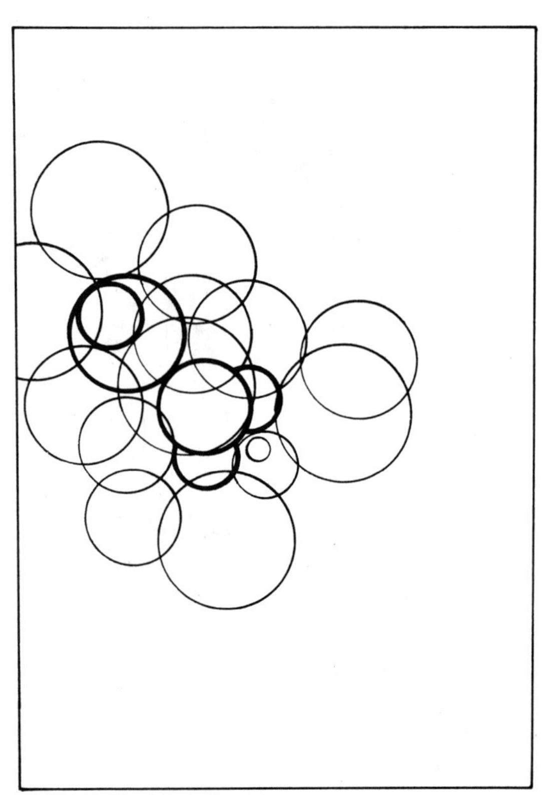

54A

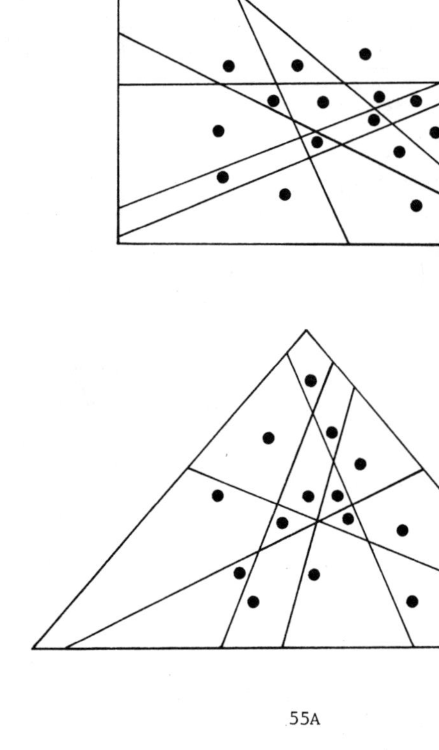

55A

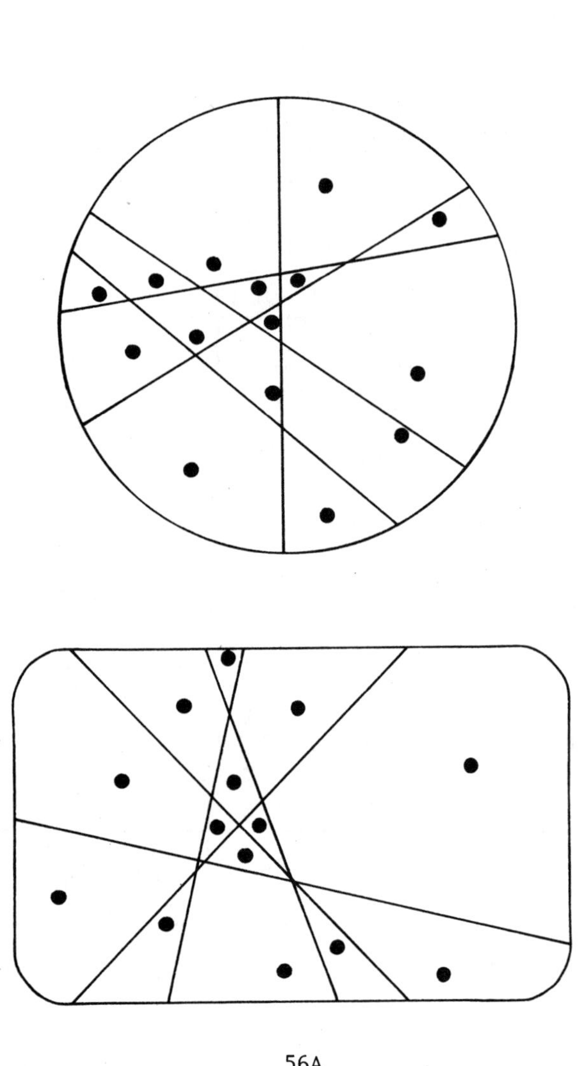

56A

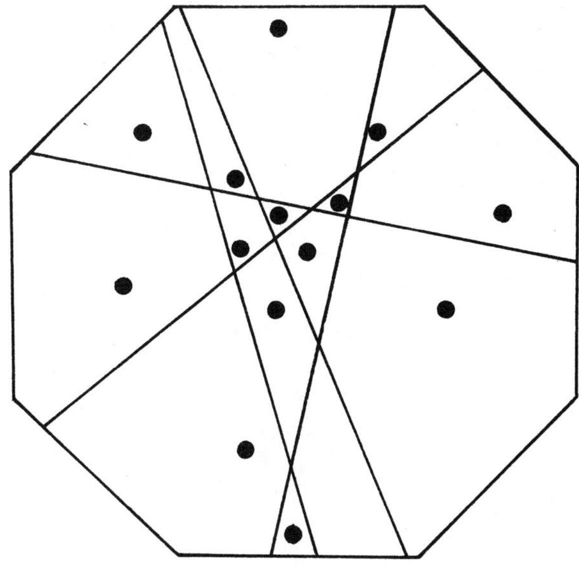

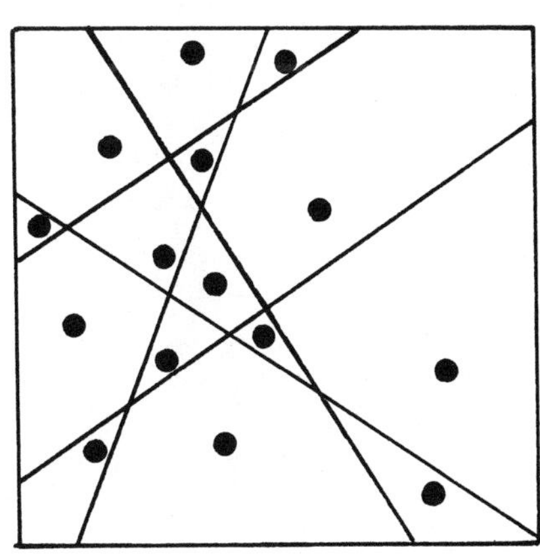

57A

Page 58A

    1 + 19 + 24 + 27 + 31 = 102
    2 + 6 + 24 + 31 + 39 = 102
    2 + 15 + 19 + 27 + 39 = 102
    2 + 15 + 24 + 30 + 31 = 102
    2 + 19 + 24 + 27 + 30 = 102
    2 + 11 + 19 + 31 + 39 = 102
    6 + 11 + 15 + 31 + 39 = 102
    6 + 11 + 19 + 27 + 39 = 102
    6 + 11 + 24 + 30 + 31 = 102
    6 + 15 + 24 + 27 + 30 = 102
    9 + 11 + 19 + 24 + 39 = 102
    9 + 11 + 24 + 27 + 31 = 102
    11 + 15 + 19 + 27 + 30 = 102

Page 58B

    2 + 4 + 19 + 29 + 31 = 85
    2 + 4 + 21 + 27 + 31 = 85
    2 + 11 + 14 + 27 + 31 = 85
    2 + 14 + 17 + 21 + 31 = 85
    2 + 14 + 19 + 21 + 29 = 85
    4 + 7 + 14 + 29 + 31 = 85
    4 + 11 + 14 + 27 + 29 = 85
    4 + 14 + 17 + 19 + 31 = 85
    4 + 14 + 17 + 21 + 29 = 85
    4 + 14 + 19 + 21 + 27 = 85
    5 + 7 + 17 + 27 + 29 = 85
    5 + 11 + 17 + 21 + 31 = 85
    5 + 11 + 19 + 21 + 29 = 85
    7 + 11 + 17 + 19 + 31 = 85
    7 + 11 + 17 + 21 + 29 = 85
    7 + 11 + 19 + 21 + 27 = 85

Page 59A

    5 + 7 + 17 + 31 = 60
    5 + 9 + 15 + 31 = 60
    7 + 9 + 19 + 25 = 60
    9 + 15 + 17 + 19 = 60

Page 59B

    7 + 14 + 29 + 34 = 84

Page 60A

    3 + 11 + 24 + 33 + 45 = 116
    8 + 11 + 19 + 33 + 45 = 116
    11 + 17 + 19 + 24 + 45 = 116

Page 60B

    1 + 5 + 7 + 27 + 31 = 71
    1 + 5 + 15 + 19 + 31 = 71
    1 + 7 + 11 + 21 + 31 = 71
    1 + 7 + 15 + 21 + 27 = 71
    1 + 9 + 11 + 19 + 31 = 71
    1 + 9 + 15 + 19 + 27 = 71
    5 + 7 + 9 + 19 + 31 = 71
    5 + 7 + 11 + 21 + 27 = 71
    5 + 9 + 11 + 15 + 31 = 71
    5 + 9 + 11 + 19 + 27 = 71
    5 + 11 + 15 + 19 + 21 = 71
    7 + 9 + 15 + 19 + 21 = 71